The five-minute writer

Exercise and inspiration in creative writing in five minutes a day

Margret Geraghty

howtobooks

Published by How To Books Ltd,
Spring Hill House, Spring Hill Road,
Begbroke, Oxford OX5 1RX, United Kingdom.
Tel: (01865) 375794. Fax: (01865) 379162
info@howtobooks.co.uk
www.howtobooks.co.uk

How To Books greatly reduce the carbon footprint of their books by sourcing their typesetting and
printing in the UK.

First edition 2006
Second edition 2009
Reprinted 2009

British Library Cataloguing in Publication Data
A catalogue record for this book is available from the British Library

ISBN 978 184528 339 1

Cover design by Baseline Arts Ltd, Oxford
Produced for How To Books by Deer Park Productions, Tavistock, Devon
Typeset by PDQ Typesetting, Newcastle-under-Lyme, Staffs.
Printed and bound by Bell & Bain Ltd, Glasgow

Contents

Introduction

This book grew out of my desire to create new and exciting exercises for my creative writing students. I also wanted to open doors in their minds, to encourage them to explore the power and possibilities of the written word. During the 17 years I've been running writers' workshops, I've become fascinated by the connections between fiction and other disciplines, psychology in particular. Could psychology provide answers to the questions all writers ask, such as: 'Where do ideas come from?', 'Why have the same basic plots survived since the beginning of time?', 'Can I learn to think more creatively?'

Since both psychology and fiction are dedicated to exploring the human mind, I set about exploring the links while I was studying for my degree in psychology. This proved fruitful. While Jungian studies gave me insight into the archetypal nature of fiction, cognitive psychology helped me to understand how the brain works and how it's possible to model the thought processes of creative geniuses. We can't all be geniuses. What we can do is to practise the kind of thinking that has been shown to foster creativity. I devised exercises to do precisely that.

I was also getting answers to many of the problems that beset beginner writers. For example, I learned that the reason it's so difficult to find the right words to elicit emotion in a reader is that emotions are experienced in an area of the brain that is dumb. Typically, we do not intellectualise emotions. We *feel* them. It's only when trying to convey our emotions to others that we struggle with words. And in an effort to convey this feeling, we find that all we can describe are the physical symptoms – the pounding heart and the sweaty palms. I looked at ways to ditch the sweaty palms.

My research widened to include other disciplines – linguistics, art, film, and advertising, many of which were a rich source of ideas. I found nuggets of gold in unlikely places. A sociological study into the flight-training techniques of Delta Airlines, whose cabin crew have to deal with 'difficult' passengers, was the inspiration for an exercise designed to help writers deal with dislikeable characters.

This book brings the fruits of my research together. It's designed to inspire you to write – even if you only have a few minutes to spare. Each chapter offers you a writing-related discussion followed by a five-minute exercise. Five minutes a day spent on an exercise is one of the most effective methods I know to explore your potential and develop self-discipline. The book will help you to:

◆ Access your inner self, the personal memories that reflect universal patterns of the total human 'story'.
◆ Develop a writing routine.
◆ Understand the nature of fiction as a cultural product.
◆ Recognise life as an inexhaustible source of story ideas.
◆ Stimulate creative thought.
◆ Develop whole-brain techniques for 'jumping outside the box'.
◆ Remove blocks.

I hope you will enjoy using this book as much as I have enjoyed writing it for you. Dip in. Pick a page and begin your writer's journey.

The Power of Ritual

I like bars just after they open for the evening. When the air inside is still cool and clean and everything is shiny and the bar-keep is giving himself that last look in the mirror to see if his tie is straight and his hair is smooth. I like the neat bottles on the bar back and the lovely shining glasses and the anticipation. I like to watch the man mix the first one of the evening and put it down on a crisp mat and put the folded napkin beside it. I like to taste it slowly. The first quiet drink of the evening in a quiet bar – that's wonderful.

Raymond Chandler, *The Long Goodbye*

At first sight, this is a strangely uneventful piece of prose. Raymond Chandler's novels are usually regarded as masterpieces of slick-talking and fast action. So, what's happening here? What's it all about?

It's about ritual and its significance to us as human beings. When we think of rituals, the first things that come to mind are things like religion or festivals, but a ritual can be anything that we always do in a particular way. American market researchers have discovered that late-night ice cream eating has ritualistic overtones, with people often using a favourite bowl and spoon. When a teenage girl brushes her hair one hundred times every day, that's a ritual. Making coffee is a ritual, particularly if you have one of those fancy cappuccino machines.

1

Rituals add structure to our lives. Some give us pleasure and part of that pleasure is the anticipation. Note how Marlowe, the viewpoint character in the extract, likes to taste his first drink of the evening s-l-o-w-l-y, savouring the pleasure. Note all the sensuous detail: the cool air, the shining glasses, the crisp mat, the quiet bar. Those details add atmosphere and enable us to share the pleasure. In an uncertain world, rituals provide an edge of comfort and stability.

Advertising agencies exploit this phenomenon in order to make people feel warm and receptive to their products. One car commercial, for example, featured a man and a woman and their different attitudes to the car that they share. The woman likes the car tidy. She impatiently removes a cassette from the deck and bundles a spilt packet of sweets into the glove compartment before driving off. Later, when the man takes possession, he replaces the tape, retrieves his sweets and pops one in his mouth. He smiles. Those are rituals.

In a similar way, writers can use rituals and ritualistic behaviour to create a bond or a bridge between the readers and the fictional world contained in the novel. Take another look at the Chandler extract. The preceding chapter ends like this:

> *He would have told me the story of his life if I had asked him. But I never asked him how he got his face smashed. If I had and he told me, it just possibly might have saved a couple of lives. Just possibly, no more.*

This is outside the experience of most readers. Most of us, however, have visited a bar and experienced the pleasure of a first drink. Although it's fiction, the scene has its own truth. Everyone can relate to it. As a result, that truth transfers itself to the book as a whole.

THE EXERCISE

Think about the rituals and ritualistic behaviours in your own life. A ritual can be anything that involves a fixed routine or sequence of behaviours. Try starting with a creative search to jump-start your ideas. Then, write for five minutes on your chosen ritual. Remember that the most effective way of getting it across to the readers is to make the writing simple, but graphic. Readers don't necessarily have to be familiar with your particular ritual but they must be able to relate to it.

What Are You Waiting For?
Make a List

Think of all those odd minutes in the day you spend waiting for
something: a kettle to boil, traffic to clear, trains to arrive,
entertainments to start, etc. And what about people: the dentist,
the doctor, the optician, the supermarket check-out operator, the
post office clerk, the waiter, the waitress, the children, the
children's teacher? All these people keep you *waiting*. The
individual slices of time may not be long, but if you add up those
minutes, you may be surprised at how much you lose. Next time
you find yourself waiting, start a list. I'm not talking about
shopping lists but lists you can use as catalysts for your writing,
words and thoughts that have meaning for you. The beauty of lists
is that they fit into the cracks of your day and you will find that
many of the exercises in this book make use of lists. You can start
and stop as often as you want. And at the end, you have
something to show for those lost chunks of time.

THE EXERCISE

To get you into list-making mood, here are some ideas.

◆ List your pet hates/irritations.

◆ List what you'd grab if your home was on fire.

◆ List some positive things about yourself.

◆ List your favourite childhood books.

◆ List your wishes.

◆ List the things you could never forgive.

◆ List your worries.

◆ List those feelings you'd rather not deal with.

◆ List some metaphors for sunset. The sunset looked like ...

◆ List the best presents you ever received.

◆ List some smells that have special meaning for you.

◆ List the things in your wardrobe you never wear.

◆ List the people you admire.

◆ List what you'd do if you won a million pounds.

◆ List some things you'd change about yourself if you could.

3

Playing Tag in the Schoolyard

Take a look at the above 'picture'. What do you see? Nothing much? In fact, this is a copy of a sheet of paper produced during a psychological experiment into creativity (Getzels and Jackson (1962) *Creativity and Intelligence: Explorations with Gifted Students*). The participants, all children, were asked to draw a picture entitled 'Playing Tag in the Schoolyard'. Most of the children filled their pictures with lots of details. They drew school buildings and added labels. The child who produced the above picture returned the blank sheet of paper with the title changed to 'Playing Tag in the Schoolyard – During a Blizzard'.

The experimenters considered this child to be a more creative thinker than those who had completed the assignment along traditional lines. Whether anyone would be willing to pay good money for her artistic achievement is another matter. However, one thing is true. In jumping outside the box, this child demonstrated her ability to free herself from the specific details of instructions and yet still produce something that met the brief.

As writers, we, too, struggle to free ourselves from creative ruts. All the stories in the world have already been told, and in many different forms. Joseph Campbell writes in *The Hero with a Thousand Faces*:

> *The latest incarnation of Oedipus, the continued romance of Beauty and the Beast, stand this afternoon on the corner of Forty-second Street and Fifth Avenue, waiting for the traffic light to change.*

If we want to create something fresh, then, what is the answer? If you are tempted to say 'Produce a book with blank pages' you may be surprised to learn that this has already been done. The book (which I found in the wedding gift section of a posh kitchen store) is entitled *What Men Understand About Women*. I have no idea whether it became a best-seller, but I'd hazard a guess that quite a few people bought it as a joke.

The bottom line here is that innovative products – be they wedding gifts, art, or popular novels – begin with innovative thinking. The good news is that, like all thought processes, we can train ourselves to get better at it. Indeed, research into the characteristics of highly-creative people reveals that creativity is not a single attribute. Rather, it is a combination of attributes, including – among others – fluency, flexibility, and originality. There are many exercises in this book designed to target these different aspects of creativity, and if you practise them regularly they will work for you.

Let's focus on *originality*. This is characterised by the ability to come up with ideas that are statistically unusual. Easier said than done? The good news is that you can train yourself. Psychologists have found that people who regularly come up with original ideas are also good at 'remote association', meaning the ability to form connections between things that appear to have no previous association and are remote from each other in time and/or space. This, by the way, is the thought process behind the creation of metaphor. For example, when poet Craig Raine wrote that a crescent moon at morning 'fades like fat in a frying pan', he was making a remote association between the moon and a piece of lard. The following exercise will get you started on a few remote associations of your own.

THE EXERCISE

Make a list of concrete nouns. By concrete, I mean things that are visible. Fish, tree, fire and comb are concrete nouns. Wealth is not. Nor is hunger or disappointment. Now, take the abstract noun, *life*, and try forming remote associations between it and each one of your concrete nouns. Ask yourself in what way, or ways, life might be compared to your chosen noun. Word your comparison in this way:

Life is like ...

For example, if one of the words on your list is handkerchief, you might come up with something like this:

> Life is an old-fashioned handkerchief. It starts out all starched and new in a cellophane pack, but when you've removed it, it doesn't seem as substantial as it looked. Over time, it gets thin and limp. But with a good wash and a starch, it comes up good as new.

The person who wrote this did not consider himself creative. However, he has hit a truth. Life *is* like an old-fashioned handkerchief. It takes effort to keep it looking good, but if you're willing to put in that effort, and use the right approach (the starch) you can improve it and make a fresh start. Once you've done this exercise with life, try other abstract nouns. Try anger, happiness, wealth, and so on.

101 Uses For...

You may have seen them in the bookstores, slim jokey volumes which purport to give the reader 101 uses for everything from a bridesmaid dress to an old farm tractor. I don't know who started this. One of the longest running is *Sticky Wicket: Almost 101 Uses for a Dead Cricket Bat,* by Philip Scofield, which was first published in 1982. The most famous – and best-selling – is cartoonist Simon Bond's classic *101 Uses for a Dead Cat,* which came out in an omnibus edition 20 years after it was first published, including *101 More Uses for a Dead Cat.* I'm not quite sure what this says about our society's sense of humour. What I do know is that coming up with 101 uses for anything – live, dead, or inanimate – certainly reveals something about the creative mind of the author. It shows that it's capable of spontaneous flexibility.

Flexibility is the ability to think of different kinds of ideas. When you are flexible, your mind can hop or jump from one category of ideas to another, and many of those ideas will be quirky and fresh. For any writer who is searching for a new slant on a familiar theme, or a cunning twist to an old plot, flexibility is a must-have attribute. Without it, we are likely to find ourselves walking the same well-worn paths that lead to repetition and creative cul-de-sacs.

But what makes it so easy for some and so hard for others to be spontaneously flexible? Education, environment and culture are all implicated. Most young children have no problem seeing a cardboard box as a castle, or a banana as a pretend telephone. To them, the world is still new and they are still learning. As we get older, we know more, but we may also be limited by what we know. Psychologist Karl Duncker introduced the term 'functional fixedness' to describe the mode of thought that makes it difficult for us to imagine something familiar being used in a new way or in a different context. He demonstrated this in a now classic experiment involving a candle, matches and a box of tacks. Participants in this experiment were asked to attach the candle to a wall, so that it could be used as a lamp, without dripping wax onto the table below.

The results were interesting. Duncker found that when the tacks and box were presented as individual items, participants arrived at the solution faster than when the tacks were still in the box. The solution – in case you haven't already sussed it – was to remove the tacks from the box, tack the box to the wall and stand the candle in the box to catch the drips.

Duncker argued that people's failure to see this solution was because they were 'fixated' on the idea of the box as a container for the tacks: 'The placement of objects inside a box, helped to fix its function as a container, thus making it more difficult for the subjects to reformulate the function of the box and think of it as a support.' Once the tacks had been removed, it became a lot easier for the participants to see this alternative use and to solve the problem.

It may at first seem strange to think of creativity as problem solving, but that's exactly what it is. Innovation consists in finding new uses for knowledge we already have, or expressing that knowledge in a new way. Consequently, to be creative, we need to get past the limitations imposed on us by rigid thinking. If Tolkien, for example, had not been able to get beyond the idea of trees as trees, he would never have been able to invent the Ents, the sentient beings who guarded the Fangorn forest.

Which brings us back to those 101 uses. When we practise dreaming up different uses for a brick or a fishing net, we encourage the flexibility of thinking that helps to make us more creative.

THE EXERCISE

Write down as many different and unusual uses for the following objects as you can.

A newspaper

A cork

A wastepaper basket

A drinking glass

A button

An old ironing board

TIP: To free yourself from functional fixedness, consider all the *different* properties of the object, rather than the one that makes it fit for its present purpose. For example, a recycling bin is hollow, which makes it ideal as a container. But it does have other attributes, such as weight, size, texture, and colour. It is also non-porous, does not conduct electricity, and melts when heated beyond a certain point. However, when regional BBC ran its own '101 things to do with a blue bin' contest on the Internet, most viewers found themselves constrained by its container aspect. A home-brewing tank was one idea. Compost was another. Rather more innovative were the BBC's own suggestions which included using it as a hat at the races, a drum kit, a toboggan, a road block, something to stand on at Speaker's Corner, and turning it into Binhenge for the druid in your life.

By looking at something in terms of all its aspects, and not just those associated with its most characteristic function, you will find that the number of potential uses you can generate will dramatically increase.

HOW WOULD YOU LIKE TO BE INVISIBLE FOR A DAY?

When asked in an interview what superpower he would choose to have, Michael Crichton is reported to have answered 'invisibility'. I don't know whether Crichton imagines what this would be like. What I do know is that it's a great fantasy exercise.

Try it now and then describe your day in a short piece of writing. Alternatively, if you'd prefer to have some other superpower, feel free to explore that instead.

Pssst, in case, you hadn't noticed, this exercise is invisible, too. It's not listed in the contents and it has no number. Just my little joke.

(5)

What Makes You Happy?

While browsing in a small independent bookshop I noticed a fat little volume entitled *14,000 Things to be Happy About. Fourteen thousand* – that is a *lot*. It's also a title that's hard to ignore. Pulling out the book, I discovered that its author, linguist Barbara Ann Kipfer, started compiling the list in secondary school and it just grew and grew. First published in 1990, there are now almost a million copies of the book in print and it's even been turned into a desk calendar.

What is so special about this book? And why would anyone want to buy and read another person's 'happy' list? The answer to that is that this is no ordinary list. Rather, it's an exploration of what it means to be alive. It is quirky and creative. To take just four examples:

> *Wearing pyjamas at breakfast.*
> *A lake catching the last flecks of sunlight coming in over the pines.*
> *Sweet fresh corn and tender baby green lima beans, drenched in cream.*
> *Shadows cast by shutters against shiny white walls.*

As you can see, the author has chosen things that arouse sensation. Sunlight and shadows enhance mood. The corn and beans awaken our sense of taste. Pyjamas at breakfast suggest a lazy weekend, with all the accompanying feelings of relaxation.

Each item in this book is similarly evocative.

Not everything will strike the same chord with a reader as it does for the writer. If, for example, you've never eaten Mexican food, you might at first question how the tilt of your head as you take your first bite of a taco can make you feel happy. But what we can all relate to is the deliciousness of the moment before we start to eat. For Kipfer, it's a taco. For you, it might be a square of white chocolate, a Starbucks panini, or a slice of your mother's fruit cake.

As writers, we want our fiction to have meaning for our readers. Creating an atmosphere of shared feelings will help you achieve that. Feelings are universal. Making your own list of Things to be Happy About is a great way to get in touch with the 'feeling' side of life. It is also an excellent exercise in creativity. As a side effect, it may help you develop your potential. When psychologist Abraham Maslow studied self-actualisers, people like Einstein and Eleanor Roosevelt who had realised their full potential in terms of achievement, he found that one distinguishing characteristic was a deep appreciation of the basic experience of living.

THE EXERCISE

Make your own collection of Things to be Happy About. Add to this collection whenever you have a spare moment.

TIP: Divide your notebook into sections, listing a different sense in each. If, after a while, you notice that one of your sections is a little sparse, it could be it contains a sense you tend to overlook in your writing. You can then make a conscious effort to include it. In my writers' workshop, I often find that 'touch' is the most neglected sense, with some writers not being too sure exactly what it is. If you think of textures, the rough bark of an oak tree, for example, or the ridged surface of sand after the tide has gone out, you might think that those are visual things. However, most of us learn about texture by touching it. Roughness isn't really rough until you've felt it with your skin. Similarly, the ridged surface of sand only becomes meaningful when you squelch across it in bare feet.

6

No Time to Write?

A student in my writer's workshop recently complained that although she desperately wanted to write, she always found herself doing something else instead. 'It's finding the time,' she said. 'There just doesn't seem to be enough of it.'

This is a common problem. It's also a block. Successful writers are not usually people with time to fill. Successful writers are people whose need to write is greater than – or at least as great as – their need to do other things. Scott Turow was an attorney in a big-city law firm when he decided his urge to be a writer was too great to ignore. He wrote his first published novel, *Presumed Innocent,* as he commuted to his office every morning on the 7.39 a.m. Chicago and North Western train.

Consequently, when aspiring writers use lack of time as an excuse, it often suggests that there's another deeper reason underlying their problem. This may be something of which the writers themselves may be unaware.

If you have this problem, try asking yourself what you have to gain from *not* writing. Everything we do in life has a pay-off on some level. This even applies to destructive or self-defeating behaviour. Take, for example, a woman – we'll call her Brenda – who blames her husband and family for curtailing her ambitions. If only she hadn't married a dominating man and had five children, she'd have been able to pursue her dream of becoming a marketing executive. It might be reasonable to ask here why, if

Brenda was so keen to be a career woman, she married a man who told her what to do. All becomes clear when the children grow up, and a friend persuades Brenda to look for a job where she can work her way up. Unfortunately, Brenda now discovers she's agoraphobic and can't leave the house.

This exposes the root of Brenda's problem. Contrary to her protestations, marriage and children actually protected her from getting into situations with which she couldn't cope. Once that 'restriction' was removed, she was forced to invent another. Now, apply this to writing. Some people may be 'too busy' because what they really enjoy about writing is the idea of it. Thus, not writing relieves them of the need to face reality. Others may simply be afraid of failure. This is a reasonable fear. Dreams are precious and none of us want to have our dreams destroyed. If we can preserve the dream, fondly imagining that we, too, could be Stephen King or J. K. Rowling (if only we had the time) that's the pay-off.

For my student, the underlying reason for not writing – which she discovered by doing the exercise which follows – was her feeling of guilt at doing something for her own enjoyment. In her childhood, she'd been taught that she must finish her work before indulging in pleasure. As a result, she had what practitioners in transactional analysis call an 'until' script:

'After I retire, *then* I'll be able to travel'.
'OK, I'll come out for a drink, but first I have to finish the washing-up.'

What stands between you and your ability to sit down and write? Whatever it is, the following exercise will help you overcome it.

EXERCISE

Step 1. First, identify some thoughts that keep you from your goal. For example, you might like to complete the following sentences:

- I am not writing because ...
- The reason I can't overcome this is ...
- A benefit I am getting from not writing is ...

Step 2. Having identified your blocks, you now need to rework the sentences so that you turn them into positive affirmations. For example, if the reason you gave for not writing was lack of time, you might say: 'I now find that I do have time to write.'

If you find yourself resisting or 'arguing' with the affirmation, don't worry. Simply write down that response, too, or whatever else occurs to you. What we're doing here is making it less easy for your unconscious defences to hide the real reason for your problem from you. Until it's in your conscious mind, you can't deal with it on a conscious level.

Step 3. Take each response and reword it in the same positive way as you did before. Again wait for the response. Remember that every time your response conflicts with your affirmation, it is a thought you want changed. Work with one affirmation at a time. Depending on how deep your resistance, you will gradually find that this affirmation and counter-affirmation process results in a breaking down of barriers. For example if, when you get down to the nitty-gritty, it *is* failure that scares you, you might write the following affirmation: 'Failure doesn't bother me. It's just one step on the road to success.'

Finally, finish with another affirmation: 'Affirmations help me to overcome my blocks.' Incidentally, after doing her affirmations, my student made a contract with herself to write for five minutes every day, even when there were other things she felt she ought to be doing. Her self-discipline paid off. She has now had some of her work broadcast by the BBC.

Rediscovering Your Child's Eye

In Delia Ephron's *Hanging Up*, Eve comes home to find her recently-divorced father entertaining a woman called Esther on the patio.

> *She was the receptionist at our dentist's. She'd been the receptionist forever. Her hair, an assortment of browns that would be very attractive on a puppy but was unlikely on a person, was piled on top of her head in large loopy curls, and she had frosted orange polish on very long nails. I had always viewed them with wonder while she filled in the card for my next appointment.*

Can you see Esther? If nothing else, you'll remember Eve's description of her nails and that frosted orange polish. For writers, the physical act of seeing is even more vital than the ability to think of a plot – and it's often neglected. Remember the first time you saw snow as a child? Magical, right? By the time most of us reach adulthood, our world is familiar and we don't really see ordinary things any more. We register what we actually need to know and that's it. Sometimes not even that. I know someone who bought a pair of shoes from Marks & Spencer and didn't notice for two weeks that the left shoe was slightly different in style from the right.

It happens – and what the hell, it's amusing at dinner parties. If we want to be fiction writers, however, we need to rediscover that child's eye. In fact, what we need to do is to cultivate an artist's eye, to be aware of all those little details the ordinary person overlooks: the grub on a lilac leaf, the stain of coffee on a sugar cube, the clump of groundsel growing up through tarmac. These are the things that help to give fiction its illusion of reality.

But visual details do more. In the mind of the reader, a carefully-chosen detail has the power to magically reconstitute the environment of which it is part. In one of Alan Bennett's *Talking Heads* monologues, for example, three characters visit a cafe:

> *And the whole place is done out in red. Lampshades red.*
> *Waitresses in red. Plates red, and on the table those plastic*
> *sauce things got up to look like tomatoes. Also red. And when*
> *I look, there's a chip in the sugar.*

That chip in the sugar is one tiny detail, yet it speaks volumes about the cafe and its patrons. Note, too, how much the colour contributes.

An exercise I like to do in writing classes is to ask students to describe the flooring in the downstairs hall of our adult education centre. The replies, ranging from 'carpet tiles' to 'wood' are usually enough to illustrate the point that sometimes we just don't see what's under our noses.

Try this for yourself. Think of somewhere you visit regularly, perhaps a friend's house, with a view to describing it for a reader. Never mind the spatial arrangement – that's the easy bit. Go for the little things, the fabric on the seats, pictures on the walls, style of light fitting. Try to recall detail. A cherry wood table is very different from one made of pine or limed oak.

Now visit the place. You may be surprised at how selective your memory is, particularly when it comes to specific elements like colour and texture. Fortunately, training your eye is not at all difficult.

THE EXERCISE

Find something to look at. What you choose is up to you, but I suggest you start with a single item. It could be a spider's web, a brick wall, a cat, the leaf of a shrub, a sliced orange, a glass of water. Later, you can move on to things like buildings, streets and woods.

Once you have your chosen object, look at it intently for several minutes. Imagine you're going to paint it. Now do a word painting.

When you stop and really look at something in this way, you will begin to see things you never saw before. Be aware of pattern, light and shade. I remember listening to an interview with a blind woman who recovered her sight. I heard the wonder in her voice as she described seeing her guide dog for the first time. People had told her the dog was a 'chocolate' Labrador. To her, the dog was a whole rainbow of different browns, ranging from dark chocolate to palest cream. This is the kind of sight you want to cultivate.

You can vary this exercise by using a person as your subject, instead of an object. Next time you're in the supermarket, travelling by train, or waiting in a queue in the post office, look around you. Pick out someone and really look at them — discreetly of course. What kind of shoes are they wearing? Are their nails bitten — or perhaps painted with frosted orange polish?

Sometimes, just looking at things and noticing their peculiarities can give you ideas for stories, particularly if you're planning to write thrillers. In one Ruth Rendell TV special, for example, the detective solves the crime by noticing the back of a woman's ankles. You see, when viewed from the back, some ankles are flat, while others are bony. Check it out. I think the lesson here is that if you ever commit a crime and decide to impersonate your victim, check that your ankles are the same as hers.

I think it's a pretty safe bet we won't see Ruth Rendell out in unmatched shoes.

(8)

Turning Points

The concept of life as a highway is hardly original but it's a good metaphor just the same. And as you travel along it, you see other paths turning off. If only you could look ahead. Those side roads look enticing but they pose so many unanswered questions. Where will this lead? Should I take a chance? Maybe …

These are phrases that are good to pin above your desk because when you apply them to almost any situation they can lead to a story. In real life, it's often easier for us to stay on the high road. Fiction is different and that's part of its appeal. In fiction, through the persona of a character, readers can vicariously explore those other routes and all those risky activities without the risk of ruining their lives.

However … those characters must have a good reason for leaving that familiar track. If they decide to do something on a whim, just for the hell of it, the result is what one American editor called the Nancy Drew Syndrome. In this country, we might call it the Famous Five Syndrome: 'Gosh, Julian, there's a suspicious-looking character. Let's follow him and see what he's up to.' That's not a motive. That's curiosity and curiosity won't cut it with adult readers.

How do we give our characters a motive? We create a situation they cannot ignore. We either make the alternate road so inviting that they just have to go down it. Or we put a metaphorical bar across their path so they have no option but to alter their course.

The following extract from Susan Dunlap's *Diamond in the Buff* is an example of the latter. Set in Berkeley, California, it talks about Berkeley Syndrome, a phenomenon that occurred among university students who decided to switch on, tune in and drop out – until change was forced upon them:

> *Berkeley syndrome had blossomed in the Sixties and bloomed well through the Seventies. By the mid-Eighties, the syndromees were well into their forties. Eyes that had peered into blocks of stone and seen visions of beauty now needed bifocals; teeth that had chewed over the Peace and Freedom platform required gold crowns that part-time jobs would not pay for. And the penniless life with one change of jeans and a sleeping bag to unroll on some friend's floor was no longer viable. The need of a steady income became undeniable. And so they scraped together the money, took a course in acupressure, herbalism, or massage and prepared to be responsible adults.*

That need to pay for their health is a turning point for a whole group of people. If they want to survive into comfortable middle age they have no choice but to change direction. And from the moment they do so, their lives will never be quite the same again.

Here are some more examples to get you in the mood for thinking of turning points:

◆ An unmarried young woman finds out she is pregnant. (Roddy Doyle, *The Snapper*)

◆ A young hobbit inherits the Ruling Ring of Power whose evil can only be destroyed in the fires of Mount Doom. (J. R. R. Tolkien, *The Fellowship of the Ring*)

◆ A one-hit writer, stifled by small town life, has to decide whether to stay with his wife or follow his dream of moving to New York to make his mark at a prestigious magazine. (Garrison Keillor, *Love Me*)

◆ An ambitious young doctor has the chance to work in a medical centre that claims a 100 per cent remission rate for a particular kind of cancer. (Robin Cook, *Terminal*)

THE EXERCISE

Do a creative search using turning points as a trigger. You might start by using some of the events and opportunities in your own life and those of your friends as inspiration. It doesn't matter whether these things actually turned out to be life-changing. What matters is that they might have been. Let your imagination run riot.

When you've finished and your page is full of possibilities, choose one of those turning points. Now, write a piece in which you describe the turning point and how a character you have created reacts to it.

Alternatively, you can do it the other way around. Create the character first and do a creative search to explore all the things that could happen to that character to initiate a turning point. Then write your scene.

9

If Fate Hands You a Rattlesnake, Make a Handbag

In *How to Stop Worrying and Start Living,* Dale Carnegie tells the story of a Florida farmer who wanted to grow fruit and raise pigs. Unfortunately, the land he'd bought turned out to be a lemon – so barren and useless that nothing thrived except scrub oaks and rattlesnakes. At first he was miserable. Then he got his big idea. Instead of trying to grow fruit and raise pigs, he decided to make use of what he already had. He started a rattlesnake farm. Within just a few years, he had built up a thriving business. Not only was he selling rattlesnake skins for shoes and handbags, but he was canning rattlesnake meat, selling rattlesnake poison to make anti-venom, and pulling in tourists at the rate of 20,000 a year.

When Dale Carnegie visited this farmer, he was even able to buy a picture postcard of the place and mail it in the local village which had been renamed 'Rattlesnake, Florida', in honour of the man who 'had turned a poison lemon into sweet lemonade'.

Carnegie's dictum to make lemonade when fate hands you a lemon has since become something of a mantra in motivational circles. As with all great metaphors, it's easy to remember and it cuts to the core of what success in life is all about. It's not about being lucky or privileged, but about making the best of what you have, even to the extent of turning liabilities into assets.

In our own lives, of course, it isn't always that simple, and most of us know what it feels like to be disappointed or have a cherished dream squashed. Consequently, when we hear or read about people who *have* succeeded in overcoming personal misfortune, we are immediately enthralled. Such people are our heroes, inspirational beings whose courage and determination is a source of wonder and hope. People like Helen Keller, the woman who used her own triumph over disability to educate others; Simon Weston, whose badly-burned face became a symbol of the Falklands war; Heather Mills who lost her leg in an accident, and went on to set up the Heather Mills Health Trust which recycles prosthetic limbs to casualties of war.

In fiction, characters who manage to deny adversity a rite of passage are just as popular as their real-life counterparts. In 2003, for example, when the BBC was running its *Big Read* search for the nation's favourite books, a reader on the BBC message board explained that she voted for *Jane Eyre* because: 'I love Jane's strength in the face of adversity, her rebelliousness and the way she never gives up and always remains true to herself.'

Other examples abound in literature and film. Think of Forrest Gump, the mentally challenged boy whose guiding principle is to be the best that he can be; Jean Paget in *A Town like Alice* who sees the potential for ice cream in the tropical Gulf country; Diane Keaton's character in *Baby Boom,* who leaves her city job and ends up in New England with a small child and an orchard full of apples. To use up the apples, she turns them into babyfood, and starts a new company called Country Baby.

What unites such characters – and the real people on whom many are based – is their refusal to give up when the chips are down, and their determination to use their experience – however limited – in a positive way. As Helen Keller once put it: 'Although the world is full of suffering, it is also full of the overcoming of it.'

When you apply this principle to your own characters you're onto a winner. Readers aren't interested in characters who don't engage with their problems. Whether you're writing a novel or a short story, you need to give make your characters architects of their own fate, meaning that the story progresses as a result of what *they* do, and not just as a result of external circumstances.

Remember, too, that the character may come to a fresh appraisal of their situation. Like the man whose land was overrun with rattlesnakes, they may realise that what they originally desired is not going to happen, but that maybe what they have is better than they thought, or they may discover a new way of coping.

THE EXERCISE

To give you some practice in the kind of positive thinking you'll be doing for your characters, think about all the times in your own life when fate has handed you a lemon. For example:

- Did you once fail an important exam?

- Did you once lose some money that you never got back?

- Are there situations or people in your life that you feel hindered your development?

- Are you angry about something that happened and which is now too late to put right?

- Do you feel that if only ... everything would have been different and better?

◆ What did you lack as a child? What dreams have been crushed, what ambitions thwarted?

Write down as many things down as you can, and don't forget that you can add to the list whenever you want. Now, try looking at each item on your list in a different light. No matter how negative it might have seemed to you at the time, look for a positive aspect, something you can pull from the wreckage. Even the worst things in life have the potential to yield a positive angle if we will only look for it. You can find an excellent example of this in Susan Orlean's *The Orchid Thief*, a non-fiction book about John Laroche, the eponymous thief:

> One of his greatest assets is his optimism — that is, he sees a profitable outcome in practically every life situation, including disastrous ones. Years ago, he spilled toxic pesticide into a cut on his hand and suffered permanent heart and liver damage from it. In his opinion, it was all for the best because he was able to sell an article about the experience ('Would You Die for your Plants?') to a gardening journal.

After you've looked at situations in your past, you might like to think about some current problematic situations, ones that are not too late to do something about. How might you see these differently? Or, to put it in Carnegie's terms, turn lemons into lemonade?

10

Rewriting Clichés

In real life, most of us speak in clichés. When we're nervous, we have *butterflies in our stomachs*. When the weather turns bad, our hands feel *cold as ice,* and we may walk through fog *as thick as pea soup*. Our enemies are *hard as nails*, but our close friends are *solid as the Rock of Gibraltar*. In disconcerting circumstances, we feel like a *fish out of water,* but we're *quick as lightning* when the occasion demands it. And when things go *pear-shaped*, our *hearts sink* – sometimes *like lead.*

The italicised phrases are all tired old expressions. They sounded great when they were minted, but overuse has exhausted them. Now they're just shorthand. When you write that someone was 'as cool as a cucumber', everyone knows what you mean, but the simile is too stale to create an image, which is, after all, the purpose of metaphor.

But if cliché is such a part of everyday life, what's wrong with using it in fiction? In fact, there's nothing intrinsically wrong with it. Indeed, if our characters didn't use the occasional cliché in their dialogue they wouldn't seem real. However, chances are that the writer who writes in cliché, is also *thinking* in cliché, and that is a problem. Keep in mind that clichés are substitutes for original thinking. Consequently, each time you use a cliché, you are also missing an opportunity to intensify the reader's experience. Fresh imagery delights. It also contributes a lot to the mood of the story. In the following examples, see how the authors' choice of imagery sets the tone:

It was a lovely night. Venus in the west was as bright as a
street lamp, as bright as life, as bright as Miss Huntress's
eyes, as bright as a bottle of Scotch.

(Raymond Chandler, *Trouble is my Business*)

A frown appeared on Mr Bunting's face. Normally, it
resembled that of an amiable vulture. He now looked like a
vulture dissatisfied with its breakfast corpse.

(P. G. Wodehouse)

Her final illness was mercifully quick, but harrowing. Cancer
tore through her body as if it were late for an important
meeting with a lot of other successful diseases.

(Will Self, *The Quantity Theory of Insanity*)

The ocean could be capricious. It reminded her of a cat at
play. Soft paws concealing claws.

(Alice Miller, *Swimming*)

The creation of sparkling metaphors and similes depends on being able to see things in terms of specific qualities, without being too influenced by the whole. For example, if we say that someone charges around *like a bull in a china shop*, the quality we're using for the comparison is the bull's clumsiness. Other aspects of bulls – their cloven hooves, their tails, the ring through their noses – are pretty much irrelevant for this particular simile. Every thing (and every person) has a host of different qualities. The trick is to find that comparable quality in something that may otherwise be very different.

To help break yourself out of cliché, take the following worn-out expressions and replace the words in italics with new similes of your own.

flat as *a pancake*

good as *gold*

faster than *a bat out of hell*

charging around like *a bull in a china shop*

slow as *a snail*

pretty as *a picture*

as hard to find *as a needle in a haystack*

hard as *nails*

meek as *a lamb*

white as *a sheet*

silent as *the grave*

cold as *ice*

One Minute – One Sentence

To become a writer, you need to write. And five minutes every day is better than 35 minutes – or even two hours – at the weekend. That is, after all, the premise of this book. But the truth is that we all have days when even five minutes is too much to find.

All is not lost, however. If you write just one sentence every day, you are still training your brain to produce something on demand, and on a regular basis. We all have time to write a single sentence, and that could be the trigger for a longer piece. It doesn't have to be a stunning sentence. Raymond Carver once explained how the process worked for him: 'For several days I'd been going around with this sentence in my head: "He was running the vacuum cleaner when the telephone rang." I knew a story was there and that it wanted telling … I made the story just as I'd make a poem; one line and then the next, and the next. Pretty soon I could see a story, and I knew it was my story, the one I'd been wanting to write.'

It works for novels, too. Stephen King's uncut version of *The Stand* is over 1,000 pages long and as thick as a telephone directory, yet as King says in his preface:

When asked, 'How do you write?' I invariably answer, 'One word at a time', and the answer is invariably dismissed. But that is all it is. It sounds too simple to be true, but consider the Great Wall of China, if you will: one stone at a time, man.

That's all. One stone at a time. But I've read that you can see that motherfucker from space without a telescope.

Here are some sentences to set your mind buzzing.

♦ Death seems to have solved my posture problems – and improved my muscle tone. (Martin Amis, *London Fields*)

♦ She had never heard of mixed feelings. (Jeanette Winterson, *Oranges are not the only Fruit*)

♦ The more I thought about my gloves and my yellowness, the more depressed I got. (J. D. Salinger, *The Catcher in the Rye*)

♦ I seldom discover feet protruding from the top of my washing machine ... (Tamar Myers, *Thou Shalt not Grill*)

♦ I haven't killed anyone for years ... it was just a phase I was going through. (Ian McEwan, *The Wasp Factory*)

♦ I met him in the street called Straight. (Mary Stewart, *The Gabriel Hounds*)

THE EXERCISE

Take one minute to write a single sentence. Don't think too hard and don't worry if it doesn't make sense. Here are some ideas to get you started:

- Write a sentence about an animal.
- Write a sentence about an inanimate object.
- Write a sentence about how you're feeling right now.
- Write a dull sentence (it might be harder than you think).
- Write a sentence about sex.
- Write a sentence beginning with a name.
- Write a sentence about the weather.
- Write a silly sentence.
- Write a sentence about a place.
- Write a sentence about a habit.
- Write a sentence about yourself.
- Write a sentence beginning with an expletive.
- Write a sentence about water.
- Write a sentence about love.
- Write a sentence beginning with 'How ...'.
- Write a sentence about a season (winter, spring, summer, autumn).
- Write a sentence about death.

(12)

The Name of the Game

In every James Bond story, there comes a point where 007 introduces himself. Usually he's just done something to attract attention, like beating the baddie at roulette, jumping out of an aircraft, or nonchalantly tossing a mob of musclemen through a window. 'Good evening,' he says with customary cool. 'The name's Bond, James Bond.'

Bond is known the world over as one of literature's most popular characters, yet according to a television documentary on Ian Fleming, 007's name was a serendipitous accident. When he began the first Bond book, *Casino Royale,* he was living in Jamaica: 'I wanted a really flat quiet name and one of my bibles out here is James Bond's *Birds of the West Indies.* I thought, well, that's a pretty quiet name so I just took it and used it.'

From ornithologist to dashing spy in one easy leap of faith. Nowadays, it's hard to imagine James Bond as anyone other than 007. The name fits the character and the character fits the name. For many writers, though, getting the right name isn't quite such plain skydiving. Indeed, Daphne du Maurier never managed to think of a name for her heroine in *Rebecca.* Others find that characters won't talk if they have the wrong name. In Elmore Leonard's *Bandits,* for example, Frank Matise's lips were zipped until Leonard turned him into Frank Delaney. Then he couldn't shut him up. As Leonard puts it: 'He wasn't comfortable in the other name.'

So, is dreaming up names an art or a science? Perhaps a little bit of both. Albert Mehrabian, an American psychologist specialising in the field of non-verbal communication, has found that names have a significant influence on how people perceive each other: 'Experimental findings show that people with desirable or attractive names are treated more favourably by others than are those with undesirable or unattractive names. Also, persons with undesirable or unattractive names tend to be handicapped in their personal, social, and work-related activities.' This is worth remembering if you decide to give one of your characters an unusual name. When Mehrabian asked people to score names from 1–100, according to how intelligent, successful and creative they thought a person of that name would be, 'John' received an average score of 98, whereas 'Knut' got 11. Ouch! (*Baby Name Report Card: Beneficial and Harmful Baby Names*, Albert Mehrabian, Ph.D.)

But names influence more than how people perceive others. They also help to define how people perceive themselves. For example, British psychologist Helen Petrie found that girls who were given more feminine names were more feminine in their personalities, while those whose names embodied unisex or masculine connotations were more assertive.

Of course, the notion of what is desirable does vary according to time and culture. My mother was christened Gladys Rita after two glamorous film stars of the 1920s. The names soon lost their gloss and my mother became Paddy – until she moved to Ireland where she had to resort to Patricia to avoid confusion over gender. Similarly, in Great Britain, Kylie may evoke images of an exotic pop idol, but in Australia it's as sheep-shearing plain as Katie or Sue.

Fortunately, when it comes to choosing names for our creations, writers have it a lot easier than parents. We simply have to select something that will work within the context of the story. Who cares what happens 20 years down the line? If you're looking for ideas, the Internet has a dazzling array of interesting sites. Whether you want the latest top 50 boy's Christian names, mediaeval Jewish names, women's names in early 13th century England, Dutch surnames, Irish names, Saints' names, or simply the meaning of names, the search engines will find it for you. To generate your own unique combinations of first name and surname, try the following exercise. It's easy and fun and you will get results in record time.

THE EXERCISE

You'll need a sheet of lined paper and a pair of scissors. Start by folding the sheet of paper in half lengthways in order to make a crease mark down the centre. Next, make a list of everyone you know, friends, relatives, and people at work. Include your own name if you like. Print first names down the left side of the crease, and surnames down the right. If you run out of ideas, try the cast lists of films, famous authors, pop stars, or even fictional characters. It doesn't matter whether you like the name or not. Indeed, for this exercise, it's good to have a mixture.

When you've finished, cut the paper in half down the crease. You now have two independent lists, one of first names, and one of surnames, which you can use to experiment with fresh combinations. Obviously, the longer your original list, the more combinations will be possible, but even if you can only think of six, you're still looking at an instant collection of 30 new names. I did this with some cast members of *The Lord of the Rings*, and came up with some very interesting 'new' people. Try it yourself now:

Orlando	Bloom
Sean	Astin
Miranda	Otto
Elijah	Wood
Ian	McKellen
Christopher	Lee

Of course, not all combinations work. Ian Otto sounds a bit odd. But how about Miranda McKellen? Orlando Lee? Or Sean Wood?

If you like the idea of a more permanent instant name generator, use index cards. Print a single name on every card and keep them in separate piles, one for first names, the other for surnames. When you need a new name, shuffle the piles and pick two at random. The beauty of this method is that you can add to it as and when a new name comes your way.

Turning Stains Into Stories

Five centuries ago, Leonardo da Vinci wrote this in his notebook:

I cannot forbear to mention among these precepts a new device for study which, although it may seem but trivial and almost ludicrous, is nevertheless extremely useful in arousing the mind to various inventions. And that is, when you look at a wall spotted with stains or with stones of various patterns, if you have to invent some setting, you may be able to see therein a resemblance to various landscapes, beautified with mountains, rivers, rocks, trees, or again you may see battles and figures in action or strange faces and costumes and an endless variety of objects which you could reduce to complete and well-drawn forms. And these appear on such walls confusedly, like the sound of bells in whose jangle you may find any name or word you choose to imagine.

Well of course, you don't have to be Leonardo da Vinci to see meaningful shapes in random patterns. Young children do it all the time. A student in my writers' workshop remembers lying in bed at night terrified by the shadow of her own discarded clothes on the wall. And most of us can probably recall seeing faces in clouds, or – if you lived in old houses – damp patches on the ceiling.

This may not seem like creative activity, but it is. Just as da Vinci used his imagination to 'see' mythical landscapes on a stained wall, so did my student use imagination to 'see' monsters lurking in a pile of clothes. Of course, this doesn't mean that everyone is equally talented. What it means is that we all interpret the world through our personal perceptual filter which has been shaped and coloured by the influences and experiences we've encountered in our lives. Because children's filters are less constrained by logic and experience – well, it *could* be a monster; there *could* be an elephant in the garden – they are open to more ideas than the average adult. The ideas may seem silly or outlandish to an adult but that's only because adults know more. For us, the world is familiar. We've been there, done that.

And there's the rub. When we start to take the familiar for granted, we stop being curious. We stop asking questions and, as a result, we pride ourselves on seeing what's there, as opposed to what *might* there. Instead of monsters, we see boring piles of clothes needing to be washed. Instead of mythical landscapes, we see grease spots, and so on. If we want to see more creatively, we need to adjust our perceptual filter, bring it back to that 'childlike' vision.

But how? In his book *Creativity: Flow and the Psychology of Discovery and Invention*, Mihaly Csikszentmihalyi suggests that 'the first step toward a more creative life is the cultivation of curiosity and interest'. Where Leonardo da Vinci might see the potential for great art in a random pile of stones, the writer might see the potential for fiction in a random collection of characters, objects, images, or emotions.

An interesting example of this potential in action is *The Plot Thickens,* an anthology written to raise money to fight illiteracy in the United States. Eleven best-selling contributors were asked to write stories which included a combination of specific elements: a thick fog, a thick steak and a thick book. I particularly liked Donald E. Westlake's *Take it away* which features a cop on stake-out buying food at a burger bar.

This technique works because the brain is designed to make meaning from whatever it encounters. It doesn't know that these elements are random. It just does its best to make sense of them. It really doesn't much matter what elements you use, but triads seem to work best. Experiment. Something that always generates results in writing classes is character, setting, and object. The following exercise will get you started.

EXERCISE

Pick one character, setting and object from each of the columns. To make your choice random, I suggest you copy each word onto a separate card or piece of paper. You'll then have three little packs of 'cards' which you can add to yourself. Whenever you want an idea, shuffle the cards. Write for five minutes, using the elements to trigger your creative brain into combination mode.

doctor	lake	bottle of scent
twins	farm	umbrella
hitchkiker	hotel	letter
gardener	supermarket	camera
thief	museum	chess set
single parent	school	wheelchair
fortune teller	cinema	teddy bear

Unfinished Sentences

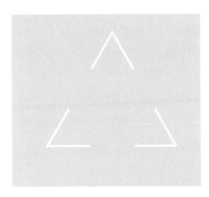

One thing at which our brains excel is what Gestalt psychologists call the law of 'good form', which is really a fancy way of saying that it will try to make sense of things even when presented with incomplete information. Take a look at the above picture. It looks like a triangle, not because it *is* a triangle but because it's a collection of lines that seems to make most sense when interpreted as a triangle. In other words, our brain 'fills in the gaps'. This pattern-making ability is an integral part of our adaptation. Without it, all we could experience would be chaos.

Many puzzles and games are based on our brain's innate desire to organise a coherent whole from fragments of information. When I was a child and had to stay at home with a cold, my mother used to buy me 'dot-to-dot' puzzle books, which kept my mind off my runny nose for hours. Jigsaws are another obvious example, as is the perennial quiz show favourite: 'complete this well-known proverb ...' or 'identify this famous person from their eyes, mouth, nose' or whatever.

As writers, we can make use of the law of good form to get the creative parts of our brain into gear. We do this, not by sitting down in front on a blank computer screen or pad of paper, but by offering up tantalising titbits in the form of unfinished sentences. To our brains, this is the equivalent of the cocktail party canape, the in-flight pack of peanuts, the smoked salmon appetiser. Your creative juice will start to flow and before you know what's happening, your page will be filled. OK, you may not be looking at *War and Peace* – this is after all a five-minute exercise – but you will be writing and that is our goal.

THE EXERCISE

Choose one of these unfinished sentences and write for five minutes — or longer. Feel free to change the first person viewpoint to third, and insert names, if you wish.

I guessed that something was wrong as soon as I ...

The stale smell of the old rug made me ...

I always knew ...

If only ...

I love ...

As the mist cleared, I saw ...

It was getting late when ...

As the train gathered speed, I suddenly remembered ...

People don't ...

The last thing I wanted to do that day was ...

I have never told anyone this before, but ...

When I reached the top of the hill, I turned and looked down over ...

On Monday evenings, I always ...

I watched from the shadows until ...

Fill in the Blanks

This is a variation on the previous exercise. Play around with ideas and see how the sentences alter, depending on what words you choose to fill in the blanks.

She only stopped _____ when _____ .

'What is the use of a _____?' she said. 'It's not going to solve anything.'

He had not imagined that something so _____ could affect him so _____ .

As a rule, she never _____ but _____ .

And sometimes, when _____ came home from _____, Mum would be _____ .

'I'm going to buy a _____' he announced, while we were _____ .

'I need a _____' she said.

I was feeling _____ as I walked across the _____ .

He got his new _____ out of the bag and _____ .

16

Time After Time

In Guy de Maupassant's story *Bel Ami*, there is a scene in which the viewpoint character, Georges Du Roy goes to meet Suzanne, a woman who has agreed to elope with him at midnight:

> *He went out towards 11 o'clock, wandered about some time, took a cab, and had it drawn up in the Place de la Concorde, by the Ministry of Marine. From time to time he struck a match to see the time by his watch. When he saw midnight approaching, his impatience became feverish. Every moment he thrust his head out of the window to look. A distant clock struck 12, then another nearer, then two together, then a last one very far away. When the latter had ceased to sound, he thought, 'It is all over. It is a failure. She won't come.' He had made up his mind, however, to wait until daylight. In these matters one must be patient.*
>
> *He heard the quarter strike, then the half-hour, then the quarter to, and all the clocks repeated 'one' as they had announced midnight ...*

This is a verbal example of a visual technique called montage. You're probably most familiar with montage from old Hollywood films in which a series of images – autumn leaves fluttering to the ground or calendar pages blowing away – indicate the passing of time. When the montage ends, the action resumes and no one is surprised to find that certain things have changed. Maybe a child has grown up or an adult has grown old. In *Bel Ami,* however, the sequential strikings of midnight appear to slow down time, rather than speeding it up. As such they create an effect that encapsulates the *emotional* quality of time for this particular character on this particular night.

This effect is similar to Russian montage in which meaning is created through the juxtaposition of specific images. Audiences shown a close-up of an actor's neutral face, for example, perceive different emotional expressions according to whether the previous shot is of a woman in a coffin or a bowl of soup. In the above extract, as each clock strikes, Suzanne's imminent arrival grows more remote, and the neutrality of time becomes suffused with deep feeling.

Time lends itself to emotional resonance because time, like memory, is associative. Midnight and noon are particularly evocative and this is reflected in many book, film and song titles. Think of *High Noon* with Gary Cooper, *Midnight Cowboy* with Jon Voight, and – more recently – *Shanghai Noon* with Jackie Chan. Similarly, a search on Amazon turns up a dazzling array of time-related fiction, including *Seven O'Clock Tales* by Enid Blyton, *Five O'Clock Shadow* by Susan Slater, *The 4.50 from Paddington* by Agatha Christie, and *Four Past Midnight* by Stephen King.

Almost any time of day can be given deeper meaning. Remember that TV commercial in which women office workers rush to make an 11 a.m. appointment to watch a hunky man drinking cola? Why choose 11 a.m.? That's the time many of us associate with the morning coffee break. By constructing a new association between elevenses, cola, and sexual pleasure, the advertisers hoped that consumers would see cola as more than just a fizzy drink. In a similar way, writers often link emotive images with time to deepen their impact. Frederick Forsyth uses this technique a lot in *The Day of the Jackal,* the first line of which goes:

> *It is cold at 6:40 in the morning of a March day in Paris and seems even colder when a man is about to be executed by firing squad.*

Here, the coldness of the time is also associated with the more metaphorical coldness of the firing squad. Everyone understands time, even if the significance of a specific time is not immediately apparent. If you start a story with 'It was 5 o'clock on a dull Wednesday', for example, you will create a feeling of immediacy for the readers.

THE EXERCISE

◆ To get ideas for a time-associated piece of writing, do a creative search using *time* as your trigger word.

◆ As an alternative exercise, choose a specific time for your creative search – six o'clock, for example – and write a piece, using that time in the first sentence. To get ideas, ask yourself what might happen at this hour of the day? What are you normally doing? What might other people be doing? It could be the beginning of the rush hour, the time the shops close, or the time children arrive home from school. You might then get an image of your own schooldays, walking home in the autumn when the light is fading and there's that smell of bonfires in the air. Time might also mean different things on different days of the week. For me, Monday at seven is writers' workshop. Tuesday at seven is coffee in Starbucks.

17

Truly Sumptuous

Ever fancied holidaying with the rich and famous? How about the Hotel Cipriani in Venice, where a single night in the palatial Palladio suite will set you back nearly £5,000? If you'd like to rub shoulders with Madonna in Paris, try the Hotel de Crillon's Bernstein suite, named after the composer of *West Side Story*.

But what do you get for such humungous wads of your hard-earned money? A nice view, certainly. The Palladio suite overlooks the Grand Canal, while the Crillon stands on the north side of the Place de la Concorde where Queen Marie Antoinette lost her head back in 1793. Then there are the bathrooms, which are monuments to marble and flash fittings, with flattering uplighters, soft downlighters, gigantic polished mirrors, fresh flowers, upholstered furniture, and enough perfumed unguents to fill a small shop.

Ultimately, though, what you really get is something far less tangible. It's the experience. As travel writer Tom Neale says, 'A suite is still seen as a terrible extravagance, but there is something about having the very best on offer that lifts the spirits even while it depresses the bank balance.'

Indeed. Unfortunately, most of us have rather more pressing demands on our bank balances, things like mortgage payments, food and children's clothes. There is, however, one place in which experience of luxury runs as free as water from a mountain spring.

That place is, of course, between the covers of a book or the pages of a story. Here, you can create rooms whose sumptuosity is limited only by your own imagination. You can take your readers to the best hotels. You can put fresh rose-scented linen sheets on their bed, Godiva chocolates on their pillows, Tattinger champagne in their ice buckets, and fluffy deep-pile bathrobes in their climate-controlled closets. You can open their windows onto whatever landscape you choose, an ocean glittering in the morning sun, a shaded courtyard filled with the fragrance of lemon, ginger and eucalyptus, or a medieval forest in winter where the only sounds are the pattering of snow in the trees and the clink of distant sleigh bells.

THE EXERCISE

In your mind, create a room, a fantasy place in which you'd like to stay for a short while. Furnish the room in whatever style you like and include luxuries to help make your stay as comfortable as possible. Now, write about the room. Use sensory detail to bring the experience of being in this room to life for the reader. Include textures, scents, colours, sounds and tastes. If you want inspiration, check out the glossy travel or lifestyle magazines or log on to the Internet where many luxury hotels have their own website. The Hotel de Crillon (*www.crillon.com*) for example, offers you a 3D virtual reality visit in which you can imagine yourself standing in its opulent accommodation.

(18)

Last Line Triggers

'If I didn't know the ending of a story, I wouldn't begin,' wrote Katherine Anne Porter. 'I always write my last line, my last paragraphs, my last page first.'

The idea of writing your last line first may seem a bit cock-eyed, but it's a technique that seems to work for many successful authors, including those who might otherwise find endings a bit of a problem. 'I can't write endings,' says one Irish playwright, 'so if I think of a good one I nurture it like a precious little seed. Writing is a lot like driving at night – it doesn't matter if you can only see a few feet in front of your face as long as you know where you're going.'

Margaret Mitchell knew where she was going when she started *Gone with the Wind,* her panoramic story of love, war and passion in America's old south. That's because she started at the end, writing her last chapter first and working from back to front, chapter by chapter. Her final manuscript was as thick as a fruit cake, and has never been out of print.

If finding your own ending is too much, don't worry. Follow the example of Ruth Rendell whose short story, *People Don't Do Such Things*, was inspired by the last line of *Hedda Gabler*. It begins like this:

People don't do such things.

That's the last line of Hedda Gabler, and Ibsen makes this chap say it out of a sort of bewilderment at finding truth stranger than fiction. I know just how he felt. I say it myself every time I come up against the hard reality that Reeve Baker is serving fifteen years in prison for murdering my wife, and that I played my part in it, and that it happened to us three. People don't do such things. But they do.

THE EXERCISE

The following last lines all come from published stories. So that I don't influence you, I've deliberately withheld the authors and titles. (If you want to know what they are, see page 186.) Use the lines as triggers, either for an ending, or alternatively the opening scene to a flashback story to which you can return at a later date, safe in the knowledge that your ending is in place. Write for five minutes. If this technique works for you, start a 'last lines' list, and add to it whenever you find a good one.

- It had never occurred to him that a dog might be clairvoyant.
- I turned and walked away through the rain.
- It was all right.
- And so was brought to a close the complex chain of events which had begun when Theodore Racksole ordered a steak and a bottle of Bass at the table d'hôte of the Grand Babylon Hotel.
- And everything, every smallest detail, would be written on my heart for ever.
- I turned the key in the ignition and drove off.
- From hate to love – the journey was only starting.
- There should be no need to dig there ever again.
- I put out my hand to stop her getting up and I cross the room to answer the phone.
- 'Now how about another drink? I'm thirsty as hell.'

19

What If?

Two of the most frequent questions I get asked in writers'
workshops are:

- ◆ 'How can I develop ideas into stories?'
- ◆ 'How can I write an ending that works?'

It might seem as if these questions are unrelated, but in fact they
are inextricably linked. This is because the beginning of every
story contains – or should contain – the seed of its end. And seeds
only germinate on fertile ground. In other words, if you're stuck
for an ending, the bit that needs fixing usually occurs much
earlier. Often, the beginning itself is just not strong enough. Some
stories don't have enough of a dramatic situation for any ending
to work.

The key to both problems is to ask divergent thinking questions.
A divergent thinking question is one that allows you to explore
more than one path. Typically, it will begin with the words 'What
if …?' or 'Suppose …?

Using such questions, you can explore the flimsiest of triggers and
test them for story potential without limiting your ideas to any
specific direction. For example, in *How to Write and Sell Your
Personal Experiences,* Lois Duncan suggests taking a
commonplace situation and using What if …? to change one
element:

*Anne's husband comes home from work every night – but –
what if one evening he doesn't? Jane lives alone in a city
apartment – but what if she wakes one night and finds she
isn't alone? What if she hears someone breathing in the dark
next to her?*

Duncan, who writes young adult suspense fiction, used this
approach for *Stranger with My Face*. What if Laurie looks at her
reflection while brushing her hair and sees another girl's face
looking back at her? What does this mean? Suppose …

Duncan's novel is a nail-biting thriller in which Laurie uncovers
the secrets of her past and the identity of the girl who looks
exactly like her.

Another authors' favourite is to apply the 'What if …?' technique
to items in newspapers and magazines, most of which have plenty
of story seeds waiting to germinate. Take, for example, the
following *Bad Idea of the Week* item which appeared in *The
Sunday Times:*

*A teenage boy, told not to hold parties while his parents were
away, ignored the warning and threw a string of rowdy events.
But on the day that his parents were due to return the 16-
year-old began to panic about damage to the house: holes in
walls and scratches on the kitchen cabinet. Fearing he could
never fix it in time, the boy decided on drastic action – he
burnt the house down.*

To turn this into satisfying fiction, we need to develop that initial
dramatic situation. As it stands, the boy solves his problem too
quickly. Let's try changing some of the elements. What if the boy

didn't burn the house down? In fact, what if he wasn't worried about damage to the house at all, but something else? Suppose one of his visitors steals something from the house? What if the stolen item is a valuable ornament belonging to his mother – something irreplaceable? What if he knows who took the ornament, but for some reason he can't immediately reclaim it? What if his efforts to put things right only make them worse?

Film fans with long memories may recognise this as the plot of *Risky Business,* the 1980s hit that turned Tom Cruise into big business at the box office. It's worth watching just for the sight of Tom Cruise playing air guitar in his underwear, but it's also beautifully plotted, a perfect example of a situation that escalates out of control as the main character, Joel Goodson, struggles to solve his problems.

Penny Vincenzi, interviewed by Judith Spelman in *Writing Magazine,* says that all her novels start with 'What if ...?': 'What if your husband asked you to perjure yourself to keep him out of jail (which is my book *Dilemma*). What if you, the bride, disappear on the morning of the wedding (*Another Woman*)?'

Divergent thinking is concerned with investigating possibilities rather than finding a single 'right' answer – which always acts to close off other avenues. Fans of the creative training guru Edward de Bono may be familiar with the term 'lateral thinking' – a more visual way of describing what is essentially the same thought process – and neurological studies show that your brain behaves differently when you're using this kind of thinking. Not only do you activate more neural connections, which suggests you're accessing more of your creative 'compost' heap of memories and fantasies, but the pattern of activity is similar to that of mental relaxation. This helps to explain the 'aha' phenomenon, whereby you often find that ideas pop into your head when you least expect them. This isn't the Muse choosing to visit you. It's a natural consequence of giving your brain something to munch on. Divergent thinking questions encourage that internal munching. Try the following exercise.

THE EXERCISE

Take a dramatic situation, maybe one that you've read about in a newspaper or magazine, and use divergent thinking questions – 'What if …?', 'Suppose …?' – to turn that situation into fiction.

TIP: Divergent thinking is a brainstorming process in which fluency is a key attribute. Fluency simply means thinking of as many ideas as you can. Just write down anything that occurs to you, however silly. Silly ideas often have a habit of sparking something else or leading you down alleys that culminate in gold. A good tip here is to ponder your chosen situation at bedtime. Many writers find that ideas come to them in dreams – or in the morning when they wake up.

20

Gimme the Money

---

*If Wilma Bean had not been in Philadelphia visiting her
sister, Dorothy, it would never have happened. Ernie, knowing
that Wilma had watched the drawing on television, would have
rushed home at midnight from his job as a security guard at
the One-Stop Mall in Paramus, New Jersey, and they'd have
celebrated together. Two million dollars! That was their share
of the special lottery.*

Mary Higgins Clark, *That's the Ticket*

Mary Higgins Clark is fond of crafting stories around a lottery
theme. As she explains: 'Lottery tickets provide endless ideas for
plots because into whosever hands the ticket falls go all of the
winnings.' In the above story, poor Ernie gets drunk and loses the
winning ticket to an ageing floozy in a bar. We spend the first half
of the story worrying about how she's going to persuade him to
part with it, and the second half worrying how his wife, Wilma,
will manage to get it back.

As themes go, money – winning it, losing it, stealing it or making
it – is one of the biggies. In real life, it's fashionable to scorn
those who are 'greedy', but millions of us do the lottery, enter
big-prize competitions, or buy a scratch card, secretly hoping that
one day, like Ernie and Wilma, we'll strike it lucky. Our desire is
nothing new. A yearning for material riches, be it gold, buried
treasure, or the superior standard of living accorded to princes
and princesses, is a standard feature of fairytales and classical

literature. Think of *Treasure Island, Aladdin,* and *King Solomon's Mines.*

Such stories and their updated variations never pass their sell-by date because everyone can relate to them: 'It's heavy,' says the police inspector as he picks up the statue of the Maltese falcon in John Huston's movie masterpiece of Dashiell Hammett's novel. 'What is it?' 'The stuff that dreams are made of,' answers Humphrey Bogart as the cynical Sam Spade.

The Falcon turns out to be a fake and the people who have coveted it come to a sticky end – as of course they must. For the unwritten rule when it comes to being showered with riches is that no one should have it who doesn't deserve it. This presents writers with a bit of a conundrum. On the one hand, stories are driven by wants and desires, and more money does seem to feature in most people's hopes and dreams. It's fiction's role to explore such dreams but deep down we know that storing up riches is not itself a worthy goal. This is why stories that end with the main character suddenly acquiring wealth are so unsatisfying. Of course we'd be delighted if that happened to us in real life, but we can guess it's not going to. Why should a fictional character have better luck?

There are several ways around this problem:

◆ You can displace the desire for riches onto secondary less scrupulous characters, who can act as scapegoats for the reader's desires without anyone having to feel guilty about it. This was Dashiell Hammett's technique in *The Maltese Falcon,* and many other stories in which the 'baddies' are shamelessly allowed to pursue filthy lucre. At the end, when it's all whipped away from them, the reader feels that justice has been done.

◆ You can play around with the main characters' motives for acquiring wealth. In the film *Raiders of the Lost Ark,* for example, the goal for both protagonist and antagonists is the same: to find the Ark. However, while the antagonists want it because it's a priceless relic and can thus be used as an instrument of power, Indiana Jones's main interest is the Ark's historical significance. From the audience's point of view, this is a far more acceptable motive and they are able to empathise more with Indiana Jones.

◆ You can create two goals for your viewpoint character, one focusing on money or treasure, and a secondary 'real' goal that only becomes apparent during the quest.

◆ You can turn the theme on its head and start with a character who is already rich. If the characters' security comes from their money, you can then have a fine old time stripping them of their wealth, and seeing how they cope. Such characters are very popular because their plight taps into the primeval human need to feel safe. For most of us, this is what money signifies. We aren't Scrooges, piling up our assets for no good reason. What we want is the security of knowing that we have choice in our lives, freedom to do what *we* want, rather than being told what to do as if we were children. Incidentally, many children's stories tap into this theme. For example, *The Bad Beginning,* the first book in Lemony Snicket's *A Series of Unfortunate Events* starts with three children losing both their parents and control of their fortune in a fire.

◆ Another option is to have your main character decide to use their riches for a worthy cause. In Gillian White's *Rich Deceiver,* Ellie wins the lottery in the first chapter. Instead of spending the money on herself, however, she decides to secretly 'buy' her husband Malc a better job, one that will allow him to feel proud of his work and his own skills. Needless to say, Ellie's plan goes wrong and she quickly discovers that money can't buy the thing she needs most.

◆ You can engage in social engineering. An early example was Dick Turpin and his clones who stole from the rich to give to the poor. Everyone loved the highwayman figure because the targets were always people who had more than they needed, or who needed taking down a peg. The BBC series, *Hustle,* in which five expert con artists only steal from the greedy is a variation on this theme. If you like classics, you might also check out E.W. Hornung's *Raffles* series of stories, featuring A. J. Raffles, the Victorian gentleman burglar, or, for an American slant, Lawrence Block's Bernie Rhodenbarr series.

THE EXERCISE

To explore the theme of money, do a five-minute creative search, using money as your nucleus word. What are your own feelings about money? What are your attitudes to it? How about lending money? Borrowing money? What would you do if you won the lottery?

When you've finished your creative search, write 'money' on a piece of paper and tuck it under your pillow when you go to bed at night or even before a nap. The rationale behind this is that what you think of just before sleep gets drawn down into your unconscious where it will be free to simmer. For many of us, money is an emotive subject and you may find that your conscious mind censors ideas that it considers 'unacceptable'. This approach bypasses the barriers thrown up by your conscious brain, allowing you access to a wider range of material.

Note: Creative search, sometimes called semantic mapping, is the technique of writing a trigger word or topic in the centre of a blank page and using it to generate a galaxy of associated words, thoughts, and feelings. As each thought comes to you, write it down, circle it and draw lines between words that seem to be connected. Keep going until you have a large web of satellite ideas. My students often refer to this as a spidergram. Tony Buzan calls it a 'mindmap' but has trademarked the term. You can call it whatever you like. The technique itself is centuries old and it works. For more information, including some fancy diagrams and lots more resources, Google mind map.

Writing with Colour

How aware are you of colour in your writing? Colours are rich in symbolic value and cultural meanings. For example, in Western societies, black clothing is traditionally associated with power and aggression, and this association appears to have a psychological effcct on the people who wear it. Psychologists studying the effect of different-coloured strip in sports found that teams wearing black behaved more aggressively and ranked near the top of their leagues in conceding penalties. When a team switched from non-black to black strip, the switch was accompanied by an immediate increase in penalties awarded against them (Frank, M. G. and Gilovich, T. (1988) 'The dark side of self- and social perception: black uniforms and aggression in professional sport', *Journal of Personality and Social Psychology*, 54, 1, 74–85).

Of course, you might argue that this is because referees *expect* teams wearing black to be more aggressive and penalise them accordingly. However, another study showed that just the action of putting on black gear changed the attitudes of college students involved in competitive games. Wearing black caused them to choose more aggressive games from a list for further competition.

All colours are capable of activating our senses in ways we may not always be consciously aware of. Yellow, for example, is a fun colour – the food industry often uses it for the packaging of snack food and products aimed at children. Red is exciting. Green is calming.

While most writers will be aware of basic colour psychology, it's worth keeping in mind that the names used to describe colours are often just as important as the colours themselves. For an instant lesson in colour association, pick up any paint catalogue. See how many of the names have quite a tenuous connection with the colours they're supposed to represent. Looking at a Dulux colour card, for example, it's not hard to see why a deep chocolate brown is called *Indulgence.* However, it's not immediately obvious why *Snuggle up* is a sort of pinkish cream. *Medina* is similar but with a yellow tint instead of pink, while *Plaza* is somewhere in between.

All becomes clear when you see that *Snuggle Up*, along with *Soft Caress* (a deeper cream), and *Treacle Delight* (a browner cream) belongs in a collection of colours called *Modern Comforts. Medina* belongs in *Global Cultures,* while *Plaza* is in *Urban,* along with *Loft* (pale lilac), *Mezzo* (pale blue) and *Manhattan View* (a slightly darker blue). What's being sold here is not really colour at all, but a lifestyle experience evoked by each collection's assigned sensory qualities. According to the brochure, the palette of *Modern Comforts,* for example, will 'help you create a cosy, comforting feel'. *Global* Cultures with its bright blues and sandy yellows is designed to 'transport you back to memories of your journeys across the world', while *Urban's* emphasis is on calm, spacious and modern living.

To perform this magic, all the colours have names that symbolise something desirable and appealing in the customer's world. When paint is called cheesecake, apple pie or soft caramel, for example, it taps into our complex relationship with food, and our tendency to turn to it for comfort. By the same token, colour names in fiction are powerful tools for shaping the reader's experience and helping to create a specific image. Gravy-brown, for example, does not evoke the same image as coffee-brown. Consider the following two examples from Gillian White's *Night Visitor*. Written from the viewpoint of Daisy who has arrived at the parental home for a family gathering, both pieces use colour to give us subtle messages concerning this character:

> *Jessie was already here.*
>
> *Her filthy red mini had been abandoned with the door left open and litter trailing out of it – a twist of cellophane, an empty bag of Walkers salt and vinegar crisps and a browning apple core.*
>
> *Granny's awful Nissan, a sickly hearing-aid beige colour, was more carefully parked in her special place against the wall.*

Although this piece may appear objective, the disparaging details reveal rather more about Daisy's perceptions of her sister and grandmother than about the characters themselves. While beige itself is a neutral colour, sickly *hearing-aid beige* suggests that Daisy sees her Granny in terms of disabilities. Although the reader cannot realise the significance of Daisy's use of filthy *red* and sickly *beige,* both are in fact accurate reflections of her own inner state, something which becomes apparent towards the end of the story. The following paragraph tells us more:

> *All around their little town lay the heart of the English countryside, hilly lanes and hedgerows that still grow flowers in springtime. Cottages in hollows and farms on knolls. A luxurious spread of green, now turning to the coffee, chocolate and malt of winter, and wrapping-paper skies of pale blue and gold.*

Here, White has used the comforts of childhood – milky drinks and present-giving – to characterise Daisy's view of her home and its surroundings. How very different these wholesome epithets are from the rather bitter and twisted associations in our previous example. Through this simple but clever use of colour, the reader is able to recognise Daisy as a young woman deeply attached to the security of childhood, a time whose reality for her has moved into the realm of rose-tinted nostalgia.

THE EXERCISE

Choose one of the following emotions:

happiness	anger	hatred
sadness	hope	dislike
love	fear	
nostalgia	boredom	

Choose either an indoor or outdoor setting. The setting may contain people or it may be an isolated spot in the middle of nowhere. It's your call. Now, write a piece describing your chosen setting from the point of view of a character who is feeling your chosen emotion. Include lots of colour and tailor your colour descriptions to suit the emotion. *Highway grey* sounds a good deal more exciting than *street grey*, for example, which suggests a rather dull and pessimistic mood. Remember, your aim is to convey your character's emotion in an implicit, rather than explicit way.

Public Places, Private Memories

In a film made during the swinging sixties, a young Irish woman called Cass walks into a deserted seaside pub and writes on the mirror: I WAS HAPPY HERE. It's a poignant act. Married to a man she doesn't love, Cass has returned to her coastal roots, only to realise she no longer belongs. Like many teenagers in search of excitement, she once believed her future lay in the city, far away from the sleepy town where the only thing that changed was the turn of the tide. Instead, working in a London garage by day, sitting alone in a rented room at night, Cass is cast adrift from everything she loves, including her Irish boyfriend who refuses to follow her.

Now, as Cass wanders across the clean sands of her childhood, she has to come to terms with the knowledge that the past has gone. Her old boyfriend is engaged. She must move on. But she was happy here, and just being in this place stirs up her former feelings. The eponymous film, *I was Happy Here,* starring Sarah Miles as Cass, is typical of many stories in which setting, characters and experience are inextricably intertwined. The Yorkshire moor, for example, mirrors the wildness of Heathcliff and Cathy's passion in *Wuthering Heights.* Every year thousands of visitors walk the craggy fells to soak up the atmosphere.

Do they hope to see Heathcliff? Probably not, but in the imagination anything is possible. Some believe that places are capable of retaining the psychic fingerprint of people who have been there. According to John Steinbeck in *Travels with Charlie,* personality even *seeps into walls and is slowly released.* Whether you believe this or not, there is no doubt that places do have power to elicit feelings. In my home town of Winchester, for example, we have several themed bars. Go in one and you're in Ireland, in another medieval England. Walk a bit further and you can be in New Orleans. What's being sold here is a kind of imaginative nostalgia, something of which American entrepreneur Kathy Kriger was well aware when she borrowed $1 million to open 'Rick's Cafe' in the Moroccan city of Casablanca. (For pictures, see *www.rickscafe.ma/about.htm*) The original cafe appeared in *Casablanca,* the film that immortalised Humphrey Bogart as the slick-talking Rick. Kriger meticulously studied the movie to capture the detail and atmosphere. There is even a piano player willing to 'Play it, Sam' at customers' request.

It's perhaps not surprising then that many fiction writers use setting to get their imaginations into gear. 'I choose the part of the city I want to write about, and just walk around absorbing the atmosphere and getting a feel for the lie of the land,' says Maggie Craig, whose family saga novels are all set in Glasgow. 'At the same time I take lots of photographs, and write my impressions in a notebook on the spot. Once I get back home, I start what I call my inspiration board.' She then pins up a few of the photos to give her a sense of place.

Although writing in a very different genre, P. D. James finds that place is the trigger: 'For me the novel invariably begins with the setting and this has been so since I wrote *Cover Her Face.* After the setting come the characters, and only then do I give thought to murderous intentions, suspects and alibis, and the mechanics of the plot.'

This power of place to stimulate the imagination may be connected to the ways in which our brains store emotionally-arousing material. An extreme example of this is our memory of dramatic events. I was in America, queuing for breakfast, when I heard about the death of Princess Diana. Someone was holding a copy of *USA Today* and the headline jumped out at me. The image of that moment is frozen in my mind: the trays of chocolate chip muffins on my left, a man drinking coffee on my right, the jugs of orange and grapefruit juice, the packets of cereal in a wicker basket. Similarly, a great many people can remember exactly where they were when they heard about the destruction of the World Trade centre, or the assassination of President Kennedy.

Psychologists call this 'flashbulb' memory, an intrinsic characteristic of which is a detailed recall of 'place'. It could be that this is a fading relic of what might once have been an important survival facility. In evolutionary terms, it makes sense for our brains to recognise certain places. If an area was dangerous, for example, our ancestors would have wanted to avoid it in future. If it was good for food and friendly, they'd want to know that, too.

Of course, we're no longer hunter-gatherers, but it takes time for our cognitive hardware to adjust. In evolutionary terms, a few thousand years is neither here nor there. If Jung was right about the collective unconscious, this would certainly help to explain those vague 'feelings' we sometimes get in old houses, and which are the staple ingredient of romantic suspense literature. For example, check out *Light In Shadow* by Jayne Anne Krentz whose heroine can 'feel' emotions in the walls.

Even if you've never had a spooky experience, you still have evocative memories of certain places, and such memories can be a fruitful source of story ideas. We all have these private associations, and we'd be fools if we didn't use those settings in our fiction. In his wonderful memoir, *On Writing,* Stephen King talks about one of his own favourite places:

> *A block down the hill, not far from Teddy's Market and across from Burretts Building Materials, was a huge tangled wilderness area with a junkyard on the far side and a train track running through the middle.*
>
> *This is one of the places I keep returning to in my imagination; it turns up in my books and stories again and again under a variety of names. The kids in It called it the Barrens; we called it the jungle.*

To explore your own associations, try the following exercise.

THE EXERCISE

Make a list of places. Here are some examples, but you can add to them or change them as you wish.

A place where you were happy.

A place where you were miserable.

A place where you were angry.

A place where you had your first kiss/sexual experience.

A place you found exciting.

A place where you felt safe.

A place where you felt frightened.

A place where you were lonely.

A place you'd like to return to.

A place you dislike or disliked in the past.

A place you never want to see again.

A place where you felt loved.

A place where you loved.

A place where you made friends.

A place where you made an enemy or enemies.

A place where you were ill.

A place where you were shocked.

A place that inspired you.

A place where you lost something important.

A place where you felt uncomfortable or upset.

A place you'd like to live – if you could.

A place you remember from a favourite book or film.

23

Are You Too Fond of Backstory?

While writers do need to think about their character's history, readers prefer to move forward and live the story as it happens to the characters. What happened to the character in the past is over and consequently less involving. Backstory, either in the form of 'telling' (*When Moira first moved to the village in 1978 ...*) or flashback episodes (*Seeing Daniel's picture swept Moira back to that terrible day when he had stormed into the room and ...*) effectively stop the forward movement and force the readers to do exactly the opposite of what they most want.

A little backstory and a few flashbacks are fine. Most novels and short stories contain at least one or two. However, it's fair to say that some new writers are so in love with their character's history that they never travel beyond it. For them, the present exists only as a means of triggering the character's memories. One writer in my workshop had this problem. No matter what the beginning, within a very few sentences he'd be whizzing back in time. The future became uncharted territory. Instead of showing how the character coped with his situation, the story became a rambling mess of explanation.

The following exercise is designed to kill backstory *dead*, as they say in the bleach commercials. But it's also good fun because it uses a theme that's rarely out of favour.

THE EXERCISE

First get your character. Decide on sex and approximate age, but don't think of a name. Now, imagine that this character wakes up in bed and cannot remember how they got there. In short they have lost their memory. Without memory, they can't think about the past and — more importantly — you can't write about it. Instead, write about what happens next.

24

Be a Character Whisperer

Having trouble grabbing hold of a character? Perhaps the character is skulking in the shadows refusing to come out, despite all your efforts to give him or her a suitable name and a nice home. You've tried a biographical checklist and it's like trying to raise the dead, only not as interesting.

Don't worry. The answer might lie in the animal world. If you've ever been around horses or watched how real-life horse whisperers like Monty Roberts tame wild mustangs, you'll know that if you stare at the animal, try to pursue it, or look confrontational, it will kick up its heels and run. The key to making friends lies in turning away and letting the horse approach you.

The same technique will often work with difficult characters. I discovered this quite by chance late one night when I was soaking in a hot bath. I was very tired, almost falling asleep and I began to think about a character in a story I was planning to write. It was a bit windy outside and I simply imagined my main character, also in a bath, listening to the rustling of the trees outside the window. Then a strange thing happened. My character got out of the bath, wrapped a pink towel around her, and wandered into an adjoining kitchen. Huh? What was this about? I hate the colour pink, and I had no idea what she was doing. As I was trying to make sense of this, heavy steps sounded outside the (fictional) kitchen door and a man entered. 'What the hell have you done with my sheep?' he said, and the two of them began to have a row.

When I wrote my story, this scene did not appear. It wasn't quite right for my plot. Instead, I appreciated it for what it was, an insight into characters whose worlds are very different. She was a townie, he was a countryman. I hadn't asked either of them to show me the way. Just as horses will nudge your shoulder when you're not looking, so characters will perform while your conscious mind dozes. When your characters won't let you in, try the following exercise.

EXERCISE

Step 1. Relax. If you find this difficult, imagine you're stroking a dog or cat, or watching fish in an aquarium. These are calming activities which can actually lower your heart rate and blood pressure, too. Sit or lie in a comfortable place, take a deep breath and just let your body flop. Visualising a pleasant outdoor scene where the sun is warm, but not hot, where everything is quiet except maybe the gentle sound of running water may also help you to unwind.

Step 2. Now, let your thoughts drift to your character in any setting that comes to mind. Get a picture of the character. What sort of shoes is she wearing, if at all? What length is his hair? Are their clothes smart or shabby? Does the character have any kind of distinctive smell? For a few moments, just focus on the character's demeanour and don't expect anything in return.

Step 3. Now think of a really ordinary situation, the kind of that happens to us all every week. It could be a charity worker standing on a street corner, rattling a collection box under the noses of passers-by. Or maybe a lost child in a store, standing crying for its mother. Or perhaps a trip to the supermarket for tonight's dinner. Choose your situation and simply place your character in it. For example, if your character is walking down the charity worker's street, what does he or she do when she gets to the corner? Maybe she just walks on by. Maybe she stops and puts something in the box. Let the character do what he or she wants. This isn't a story you're writing. It's just a game in which you are the observer. Let the character go.

When you do this, chances are that the character will start to become their own person. You see, in fiction characters act under pressure because that's what fiction is all about. But to get your know your character properly, you need to know what they're like outside the constraints of the story. That's the aim of this exercise.

Take a Chance

In Anne Tyler's *Ladder of Years,* a woman called Ellie finds a lump in her breast. The doctor tells her it's cancer. Ellie decides to take drastic action. As one character explains to another:

> *'So, she came home and told her husband, "In the time that I have left to me, I want to make the very best of my life. I want to do exactly what I've always dreamed of." And by nightfall she had packed up and gone. That was her deepest, dearest wish – did you ever hear such a thing?'*
>
> *'So where is she now?'*
>
> *'Oh, she's a TV weather lady over in Kellerton … The lump was nothing at all; they removed it under anaesthetic.'*

In real life, we often become stuck in familiar but restrictive patterns of existence. Everyone has dreams but, when it comes to the crunch, how many of us pursue them? 'It's not the right time,' we say. 'I can't do it now. Maybe later.' Later comes and goes, and before we know it we're looking back on our lives instead of forward. For some, like Ellie, a specific incident jolts us out of our lethargy, and we suddenly realise that 'can't' has changed into 'can'.

This is the main theme of Tyler's novel, inspired, she says, by her own fascination with the 'tension between the wish to fly and the resolve to stay'. Within the pages of her book, readers can explore the consequences of drastic action, without actually having to take it themselves. Every novel offers readers this vicarious experience. And every novel and short story is an opportunity for the *writer* to take the road less travelled, to explore different lives through the viewpoint of the characters. Yes, Cinderella, you can go to the ball. You can go to the moon if you want. Ray Bradbury did in *The Martian Chronicles*. You can do whatever you want.

First, though, some practice in stretching your range of creative possibilities. Try the following exercise.

THE EXERCISE

If you've ever played Monopoly, you'll know that if you land on certain squares, you get to pull a Chance card. The card might allow you to move to another square, get out of Jail free, or you might end up having to pay a parking fine. You pull the card, you take your chance. For this exercise, create your own collection of Chance cards. On each card, put down something you would like to do, a place you would like to go, a person you would like to be. Don't worry about whether what you've written is possible. Just write it. In this way, each card will symbolise a parallel universe, in which you are free to explore things you might never do in your real life. Be as adventurous as you like:

◆ I would like to open a themed restaurant.

◆ I would like to experience what it feels like to be the opposite sex.

◆ I would like to climb K2.

◆ I would like to be really good at something.

Create another category of cards on which you have written things that you wouldn't like to experience, places you wouldn't like to go (Jail?), people you wouldn't like to be, etc.

Make as many cards as you like and add to them as new ideas occur to you. Next time you have a five-minute break, shuffle all your cards together, choose one at random and write something inspired by the card. For example, if you've pulled 'I would like to teach Pilates in Australia', imagine what it would be like to do this. How would your day be different there? Who might you meet? What would you do in your spare time? Where would you live?

For this exercise, you don't need to be writing what you know. The aim is to free your imagination and get you exploring. The writing itself will reveal gaps in your knowledge and you can, if you want, set about filling them. Research can be fun, and as someone once said, 'If you want to create a character who climbs mountains, you only need to climb one mountain, and you don't need to go all the way to the top.' Pull a card, take a chance. Who knows where it might lead?

Two-Faced Characters

Have you ever met someone you were expecting to like – and found you didn't take to them at all? Or perhaps it was the other way around, and you found yourself reluctantly beginning to like someone you were all geared up to hate?

It happens. Different people see different facets of us and we, in turn, see different aspects of them, partly of course because we're looking for things that resonate with ourselves. This is most apparent when people fall in love. How often, for example, do you hear someone say, 'Oh, we're such perfect soulmates – it's unbelievable!' when they've just met someone they think is 'the one'. Later, of course, the differences begin to show and the soulmate becomes that 'selfish bastard' or that 'unfeeling cow'.

The truth of course is that none of us has just the one face that we show to the world. As a result, no matter how pleasant – or unpleasant – we may be in specific situations, few of us are universally liked or disliked. Even if we don't particularly get on with the human world, we might have an animal who sees beyond our problems and offers us unconditional adoration.

Consequently, in fiction, the most believable characters are not always those with the strongest personality traits. Indeed, it can get rather tiresome and boring if a character doesn't seem to be able to transcend his dominant attribute. No, the most believable characters are those that offer a real-life bundle of contradictions.

Their vivid quality comes from the reader's perception of them as complex people, who are not wholly good or wholly bad. To practise creating such characters, writers need to be able to move easily between different, and opposing, points of view of the same person. Try the following exercise.

THE EXERCISE

This exercise is one that counselling and psychotherapy selection boards use to find out if prospective students are likely to be flexible in their assessment of clients' problems. A key quality for all counsellors and psychotherapists is the ability to see things from different angles, and not in black and white terms. It's a key quality for writers, too, particularly those hoping to create characters that walk off the page. The exercise will give you insight into your characters, raise awareness of possible internal tensions, and also help you to avoid writing stereotypes. For maximum effect, it's important to try it first using yourself as an example.

Write around 500 words describing yourself from the point of view of someone who likes you. When you've finished, do the same thing from the point of view of someone who dislikes you.

Doing this exercise on yourself can be extremely enlightening. Instead of being one person, you appear to be two. What one person sees as 'drive', for example, another might perceive as 'work-obsessed' and so on. You begin to see how qualities are not constants but are always open to interpretation. In fact, we are all open to multiple interpretations in the eyes of the world, but most of us manage to integrate the different aspects of our character into one reasonably well-adjusted 'self'. Under stress or when facing conflict, however – as typically happens within the context of a story – we become more aware of the tensions between these different aspects.

Once you've tried this exercise on yourself, try it with a couple of characters you've been hoping to bring to life. Try it with all your characters. You'll be amazed at how productive this can be.

Change Your Life – Buy a New Pair of Jogging Shoes

When we think of life-changing events, our minds usually drift to the biggies: birth, death, marriage, having children, and so on. Perhaps for this reason, many beginners love to include death in their fiction, as if something so momentous is bound to invest the story with extra profundity. However, life is lived in the detail, and small things often have just as much – if not more – power to bring about change. I've just been reading an article about Sarah Harrison whose *Flowers of the Field* became an international best-seller in 1980, knocking Jeffrey Archer off the No. 1 slot. Yet Harrison's writing career almost stopped dead when the awesome challenge of repeating her success led to writer's block.

The answer? When asked 'What has been your best investment?' (the article was about fame and fortune) Harrison replied: 'Buying a decent pair of running shoes 23 years ago. Jogging saw off writer's block and changed my life.' Her second novel, *A Flower that's Free,* was followed by a string of other successes and while none has ever quite achieved the status of her first, Harrison has kept writing.

Everybody's life is full of small opportunities for change, although it's fair to say that we don't always recognise their potential. Having decided to do something different, we sometimes bump along a road that's almost identical to the main one, but after a while, it begins to take us in another direction, one that would not have been possible if we'd stayed on the highway. As Anthony Robbins says in *Awaken the Giant Within:*

> *I challenge you to take a decision today that can immediately change or improve the quality of your life. Do something you've been putting off ... master a new set of skills ... call someone you haven't spoken to in years. Just know that all decisions have consequences.*

Fiction thrives on such life-enhancing steps, particularly those that allow the reader to imagine the character's future life beyond the boundaries of the story. It isn't necessary to tell it all. If Sarah Harrison were a fictional person, for example, the story might end with her putting on the shoes for the first time and beginning to run. And as she runs, she hears a small insistent voice in her head that she eventually recognises as a new central character ...

Try the following exercise.

THE EXERCISE

Make a list of some small changes you could make in your life right now. The changes don't have to be important ones. It could be something as simple as choosing a new hairstyle, clearing out your loft, or maybe reading a book by an author you've never tried. For example, if I were doing this exercise, I might list 'join a line-dancing class'. This is not because I want to charge around dressed up in Western gear pretending to be a cowboy but because I need some exercise. I get bored in the gym, karate is too strenuous and I'm two decades older than Sarah Harrison was when she took up jogging. Dancing seems to fit the bill.

But who knows where it might lead? Who knows where your changes might lead? Choose one to explore. Either write a short piece or plan a short story for writing up later when you have more time.

28

Crack the Shell

How are you feeling right now?

When I did my first training course in psychodynamic counselling, this was a standard question to help clients begin to explore their emotional reaction to difficult situations. How we feel about things is the key to learning to cope with them and we can't do that effectively until we acknowledge what our deep feelings are. If we refuse to acknowledge them ('I've washed my hands of that', 'I'm not even going to think about how much he hurt me', 'I've cut her out of my life') we effectively block the emotion that's making us anxious, but we do it by means of the Freudian defence mechanism called 'repression'.

Now, repression can be very effective at banishing difficult memories, particularly those originating in childhood, but it can't destroy them. Deep in our unconscious, unresolved hurts bubble beneath their surface scars. Every so often, a scar springs a leak. Typically, this happens when we find ourselves in situations similar to ones we've encountered before. We may find ourselves unconsciously playing out an old script, following a pattern of behaviour that helped us once but is of little use now.

To take just one example, a child from a troubled home who learned to protect herself with a tough outer shell may later find it difficult to form close relationships. Expecting to be rejected, she will find her fears confirmed, without ever realising that her attitude is the problem. Consequently, when psychotherapists ask,

'How are you feeling right now?' their aim is to uncover not just the present but also the past.

What has this to do with writing? It's my theory that many writers – published and unpublished – are drawn to fiction, because, like psychotherapy, it offers an opportunity to confront the tensions in their lives. It is also a way of exploring 'self' in a safe environment. John Le Carré, whose mother ran away when he was five and whose father was 'a frightening figure', quotes Graham Greene's remark that 'childhood is the writer's bank balance'. Le Carré's novels are scattered with broken childhoods, particularly among those who become agents or traitors: 'No childhood, most of them, that's the trouble,' says a counter-intelligence officer in *A Small Town in Germany*.

Of course, many writers deny that their stories are in any way autobiographical. This is often belied by the recurrence of themes and characters who grapple with problems dear to the writer's heart. In writing classes, we see this all the time, and writers are often amazed when I point this out to them. 'That's the third story in which you've used money as a central theme,' I said to one student. 'Is this one of your hot buttons?' She stared at me dumbfounded for a moment and then she started to laugh. 'Look at this,' she said, pulling a pendant from her neck. It was a coin.

It happens. Consciously or unconsciously, writing is a way of getting to grips with the things that matter to us. If you find yourself coming back to the same or similar theme, chances are that you've hit a rich vein. For many new writers, however, tapping that vein is easier said than done. While they may be happy to explore the territory on the surface, they may hold back from anything that threatens to reveal their own vulnerabilities.

Unfortunately, the protective shell around the author then transfers itself to the characters, who appear at best enigmatic, and at worst, unfathomable. This is not what fiction is all about. As author's agent Albert Zuckerman points out in *Writing the Blockbuster Novel:*

> *What we enjoy most in a novel are often things that can never be physically seen. The authors about whom we become passionate delve deeply into the minds and hearts of a book's characters.*

What Zuckerman's talking about here is emotional depth, the basic human needs, fears and desires that underpin our characters' motivations for acting as they do. Until readers have some insight into that emotional baggage, they can't really like the character or even begin to understand them. And we, the writers, can't begin to create characters with emotional depth if we're out of touch with our emotional raw material. Rachel Ballon, a psychotherapist who also teaches creative writing, points out that many writers have no idea how to give their characters emotions because they don't allow themselves to feel their *own* emotions: 'They remain distant and detached from their feelings and are unable to put them into their characters' (*www.writersstore.com/article.php?articles_id=311*).

That may be a little harsh. Many new writers have difficulty putting feelings into characters and it isn't necessarily because they can't themselves feel. However, having feelings and being able to *access* them on demand are two different things. Until we can learn to retrieve emotions on demand, we are going to have problems giving them to characters. Let's do some emotional homework. The following exercise is designed to help you access your feelings and give them expression.

THE EXERCISE

For one week, keep a journal in which you start every entry with these words: 'Right now, I'm feeling ...'.

How you feel will obviously vary. One day, you may be happy because you've achieved something at work, for example. Another, you may be frustrated. Another, you may be angry, and so on. The particular emotion doesn't matter. What matters is that you are open and honest about it. This is not the place to hide or ignore anything. It's a place to retrieve your emotional baggage and explore it in a safe environment.

If you've never written about your feelings before, you may find this exercise amazingly therapeutic once you've got used to it. There's also a side effect. Numerous studies have shown that writing about our deepest feelings can result in both short and long term health benefits. If you're interested in this angle, check out *Opening Up: The Healing Power of Expressing Emotions* by James W. Pennebaker, PhD whose work on stress, emotion and health is well-known in the scientific community.

For more exercises and practical techniques, try *Writing As a Way of Healing: How Telling Our Stories Transforms Our Lives* by Louise Desalvo.

29

Who's Calling, Please?

Want to write but desperate for a plot? Look no further than your telephone. Ever since Alexander Graham Bell invented the 'electrical speech machine' on 6 March 1876 – the story goes that his first call was 'Come here, Watson, I need you' to his assistant in another room – telephones have transformed communication and given fiction writers a bottomless pit of story ideas. It would take a telephone directory to list them all and even then you'd probably run out of space, but try the following for size:

The phone rings, but the caller wants someone you don't even know. Or perhaps it's a crossed line where you suddenly find yourself privy to a couple of strangers' conversations. Sometimes, there's no one there at all and your 'Hello?' echoes into empty space. It's probably one of those infuriating automated dialling systems, but who knows ...?

Three familiar scenarios that have happened to us all. Yet similar instances – with added spice – occur over and over in books and films. For example, in *Sorry, Wrong Number*, originally a play by Lucille Fletcher, but later adapted for film and television, a rich bedridden woman picks up the phone and overhears two men plotting a murder. She recognises one of the voices as belonging to her husband, and soon realises that she's the planned victim. In a rather different vein, *Memento Mori* by Muriel Spark, begins with an older woman receiving a phone call from an anonymous voice that cheerfully reminds her *'Remember, you must die.'* Soon, others in her close circle of family and friends begin to receive the same phone calls.

Different again is Robert Cormier's young adult suspense novel *In the Middle of the Night,* in which a teenage boy called Denny becomes obsessed with a psychotic mystery woman out for revenge. On Halloween, eight years before Denny was born, his father was involved in a tragic accident which killed 22 children. Every year in October, the threatening phone calls begin. This year, Denny does something his father has forbidden him to do. He answers the phone ...

It's not just phone calls. Phone hardware, too, offers lots of possibilities. Think of *Doctor Who*, in which a humble police call box becomes a vehicle for transporting the Doctor through time and space. Similarly, in the movie, *The Matrix,* Neo, Trinity and their crew have to reach a ringing phone in a booth when they want to be teleported back to their ship. In each case, the box or booth is used as a symbol of stability and – in sticky situations – salvation. In Alfred Hitchcock's *The Birds*, for example, based on Daphne du Maurier's short story of the same name, Tippi Hedren hides in a phone booth as birds fling themselves against the glass, trying to attack her while she cringes inside.

But phones don't have to be associated with terror or suspense. One of my favourite films, *Local Hero,* set on the West coast of Scotland, uses a public call box to symbolise the connection between people, places and meaningful existence. When Mac, a lonely American businessman, is sent to the Highland fishing village of Furness to negotiate a deal with the locals, a public call box is his lifeline with the outside world. Every night, he goes to the box outside the pub and telephones his oil company boss in

Houston. Gradually, however, Mac finds himself captivated by the unspoilt scenery, the pleasure of collecting shells on the beach, and a local girl. When he is eventually recalled to Houston, the phone box becomes Mac's link with the simplicity and beauty of a place he has come to cherish. The film ends with the phone ringing in the empty box. According to various Scottish tourist sites, fans of the film still phone the public box in Pennan where the film was shot, and the box itself has become a public monument.

THE EXERCISE

Write for five minutes using just one of the following as inspiration:

◆ The phone rings, you pick it up and a voice you don't recognise tells you that your lover/partner/spouse is having an affair. Write the dialogue exchange.

◆ 'If you were going to die soon and had only one phone call you could make, who would you call and what would you say?' This is a quote from Stephen Levine.

◆ You have just won £1 million in the lottery. Who would you call and what would you say?

◆ The phone rings and it's a voice from the past. Who is calling and why? Write in dialogue.

◆ You pick up the phone to make a call but instead of the dial tone, you hear someone asking for help ...

◆ You are passing a public call booth and the phone is ringing. On impulse you stop and pick it up ...

◆ You are in a cafe/restaurant/pub when a member of staff calls you to the phone. When you answer, someone says: 'I'm watching you ...'.

◆ List the most difficult phone calls you've ever received or had to make.

250 Words on Something

Australian journalist David Dale recalls the time he was sitting at his desk at the *Sydney Morning Herald* when a senior editor came by and asked a favour: 'I've got a 500-word hole on the page,' the editor said. 'Everything else is really dreary. Can you do us something funny to fill the hole?'

Dale hurriedly wrote a light-hearted piece about throwing cream pies (with very soft pastry) at pompous public figures. It was never published. The editor decided that throwing confectionery was assault – despite the soft pastry – and the newspaper didn't want to be accused of inciting violence. Later, however, Dale co-authored a book called *480 Words on Anything,* a collection of 'wild theories, idle thoughts and essential explanations' covering such oddball topics as how to protect your children from Snow White and why Australia should drive on the right.

The truth is that if you put your mind to it, you can write something about anything. I'm not saying it'll be great writing, but it's still creating something where nothing existed before and that's half the battle. The other half is freeing yourself from the pursuit of quality. It sounds like such a worthwhile aim but quality – like success – is a side effect of being involved in what you're doing. As psychologist and holocaust survivor Viktor Frankl says in *Man's Search for Meaning:* 'Don't aim at success – the more you aim at it and make it a target, the more you are going to miss it.' Try this exercise.

For one minute, write down as many boring topics as you can. In writing classes, housework used to be a popular choice, but since Channel 4's *How Clean is your House*, revealed its hidden fascinations, I'm afraid it's off the agenda.

Got your list? Good. Now pick the *most* boring of your ideas, and in the four minutes you have left, write 250 words or more. Don't worry about writing well. You have a deadline. Let yourself go and get something down as fast as you can.

Turn Your Worst Moments Into Money

'Write what you know' is common 'how-to book' advice, and while it makes good sense many new authors are suspicious of it. It sounds boring. Surely, the whole point of writing is to escape your own life and write about someone else's? Well, perhaps, but it's worth remembering that readers love to hear about things going wrong. What do you do when things go wrong in your life? Most writers I know reach for their notebooks. Why waste good material? Unlike the rest of the population, writers can capitalise on everything that happens to them, whether it's embarrassing, frustrating, or even downright disastrous. As the American author J. P. Donleavy once said: 'Writing is turning one's worst moments into money.'

For Jane Wenham-Jones, this strategy has worked a treat. Before moving into novels – *Raising the Roof* and *Perfect Alibis* became best-sellers – she wrote over 100 short stories published in a wide variety of women's magazines including *Bella, Chat, My Weekly, The People's Friend, Best* and *Woman's Weekly*:

'When I was writing regularly for the women's magazines, it became a game to make anything negative that happened to me into a plot, so that something positive came out of it. For example when I backed into someone else's headlights and caused £250 worth of damage, I wrote a story about it and earned back the money. My first novel *Raising the Roof* (Bantam) is based on my experiences of renting out property (what a nightmare!)'.

It makes sense to use your nightmares, and your other frustrations, too. After all, nobody else will – except other authors on the lookout for ideas. Keep your material to yourself, or at least in a notebook. Start a frustration diary. It only takes a few minutes at the end of every day. A great side effect is that instead of getting you down, bad events will start to look like nuggets of gold. To get you started, try this exercise.

THE EXERCISE

Complete the following sentences:

The worst thing that happened to me today was …
The worst thing that happened to me this week was …
The worst thing that happened to me this month was …
The worst thing that happened to me this year was …

The Three-Mountain Solution
to Point of View

According to David Lodge, 'One of the commonest signs of a lazy or inexperienced writer of fiction is inconsistency in handling point of view.'

Harsh as this sounds, it's certainly true that many new and not-so-new writers do find it extremely difficult to 'get' point of view. Indeed, whenever we tackle it in writers' workshops, there's always at least one person with a bewildered frown. If you're one of these people, please don't think it's a sign of stupidity. On the contrary, people who read a lot of classical literature are often the most bemused. You see, before Henry James came along with his single-viewpoint *Daisy Miller,* omniscient viewpoint was the norm. Authors acted as story overseers. Not only could they choose to withhold or reveal any character's thoughts, but they could also tell readers the 'truth' as they saw it. For example, 'Ogden was a man of considerable wealth but no understanding of his employees' needs'. Who, we might ask, has decided that Ogden has no understanding? Yes, it's the author, and the author is telling the reader. In modern fiction, we try not to do this, because it denies the readers the opportunity to decide for themselves.

Another reason why people may have difficulty understanding point of view in fiction is that it's not an innate ability in real life.

It's something we learn. The Swiss developmental psychologist Jean Piaget demonstrated this with an experiment known as the Three Mountains task. In this experiment, a child sits at one side of a plaster model of mountains. Piaget would then ask the child to select from photographs the view that a doll, placed on another side, might see. Not until nine years of age were children able to grasp that the doll's point of view was different from their own.

As adults, we do of course know that our point of view is different from that of other people. Nevertheless, if you're having trouble with point of view in your fiction, the three-mountain model is a useful visual aid for getting to grips with it. If you take the mountains as a metaphor for a scene in your story, you need to ask yourself from which side of those mountains you're going to view the scene. Imagine that character A is at one point, character B at another, and so on. If you choose character A, then you can't reveal things which can only be seen from B's vantage point, and vice versa. It's worth noting that even two characters standing side by side will still have a slightly different point of view, because if these were real mountains that's how it would be.

But where – and I know you're dying to ask this – are you? The answer to that is that your point of view will be that of whatever viewpoint character you've chosen for the scene in question. Stephen King once described this as feeling 'like I'm behind their eyes looking out'. By contrast, when an author starts describing their viewpoint character's appearance, you know that they're actually facing the character, looking at them from their own point of view. Take a tip from Elmore Leonard: 'If I write in scenes and always from the point of view of a particular character – the one whose view best brings the scene to life – I'm able to concentrate on the voices of the characters telling you who they are and how they feel about what they see and what's going on, *and I'm nowhere in sight.'*

The italics are mine, and I've used them to emphasise the importance of realism in modern fiction. Readers want to believe in your characters and that's harder to do if a writer acts as a background commentator. And just to show you that Leonard practises what he preaches, in the following scene from *Get Shorty,* Chili Palmer has gone to collect his jacket from a restaurant cloakroom. Unfortunately, all he sees there are a couple of raincoats and an old leather flight jacket that:

> *must've been from World War Two.*
>
> *When Chili got the manager, an older Italian guy in a black suit, the manager looked around the practically empty checkroom and asked Chili, 'You don't find it? Is not one of these?'*
>
> *Chili said, 'You see a black leather jacket, fingertip length, has lapels like a suitcoat? You don't, you owe me three seventy-nine.' The manager told him to look at the sign there on the wall. WE CANNOT BE RESPONSIBLE FOR LOST ARTICLES. Chili said to him, 'I bet you can if you try. I didn't come down to sunny Florida to freeze my ass. You follow me? You get the coat back or you give me the three seventy-nine my wife paid for it at Alexander's.'*

The viewpoint character here is Chili. We experience the scene through Chili, and everything we learn comes from his thoughts, his actions and his speech. Who's decided that the flight jacket must've been from World War Two? Chili. There's no authorial intrusion, no 'Chili was a slick-talking guy who didn't believe in taking no for answer'. If that's the conclusion we come to, we've come to it by being with Chili on his side of the mountains. Now, see how you go with the following exercise.

THE EXERCISE

Last year, an elderly woman drove her car through the front entrance of my local supermarket, demolishing a children's ride, a passport photo booth and the side window of the coffee shop. Several people were witnesses. Write separate versions of this event from each of the following perspectives (spend five minutes on each version):

◆ The driver of the car.

◆ A checkout attendant whose till was near the entrance.

◆ A mother who had gone to get change for her small boy to have a ride.

◆ A shopper who didn't manage to get out of the way fast enough to avoid being knocked down.

◆ Another person of your choice. (Coffee shop employee? Supermarket security? Policeman?)

TIP: Remember that you're not trying to write factual accounts. What you are trying to do is to write each person's specific *experience*, and that will vary according to who they are, where they were, and their state of mind.

33

Reframing Repulsive Characters

When creating characters, standard advice is to make your protagonist likeable. Readers don't (typically) want to view the story events through the eyes of an axe murderer. However, unless you're writing really bland fiction, you'll need to include a few characters with whom you wouldn't particularly want to be friends in real life. If you're writing crime or horror fiction, you might not want to be on the same street with them – or even the same planet. This poses a bit of a conundrum. How are you to bring such characters to life? The key is identification. Wallace Hildick wrote in *Children and Fiction:*

> *To realize a character – to give it bones and muscles and sweat and blood and make it live – a writer must identify with it to some extent. Even if he is not predisposed to sympathise with a character he must at least try to see through his eyes, feel the way it feels. In this way many a cardboard devil has been endowed with a touch of humanity that has made it all the more frightening, if also more forgivable.*

Some of us may find this easier than others, depending on how unpleasant the character actually is. There are theories which suggest that all characters in fiction, whatever their likeability rating, represent aspects of our own human psyche. Indeed, some fiction has itself explored this concept. In Robert Louis Stevenson's *The Strange Case of Dr Jekyll and Mr Hyde,* for example, Dr Jekyll describes Mr Hyde as 'pure evil'. Yet Hyde

represents what Carl Jung called the 'shadow archetype', the dark
side of the psyche that we deny in ourselves and project onto
others.

To see through a dislikeable character's eyes, however, it isn't
necessary to plunge into psychoanalytic theory. All that's
necessary is a little understanding. Like writers, flight attendants
have to cope with 'difficult' people. In *The Managed Heart,*
sociologist Arlie Russell Hochschild explores a simple but effective
training technique used by Delta Airlines to cope with 'irates', the
airline's term for difficult passengers who vent their frustration on
the flight attendants. When the *Lucas Guide* ranked Delta first for
quality of service, inspectors praised the attendants' smiles, which
they perceived as genuine, rather than 'forced' or 'strained'.

To achieve this, Delta taught its crew a 'reframing' technique. If a
passenger was angry, for example, the flight attendant would
make up a story to put the anger in a different perspective.
Perhaps the passenger opened his mail that morning and found
that his wife was initiating divorce proceedings. That would be
enough to make anyone upset. With the anger now translated into
sadness, the attendant can then begin to understand the
passenger's reaction.

Similarly, when we reframe the bad behaviour of our characters,
we too transform meaning. We don't have to condone their
actions. Indeed, we may still hate the character, but we have an
inkling of why they are as they are. This helps to make them more
interesting and believable. In Whitley Strieber's *Billy,* the
antagonist, Barton, is a man for whom no normal reader could
have sympathy. He abducts young boys. To stop him becoming a
caricature of evil, the author writes certain passages from Barton's

viewpoint. In the following excerpt, we are with him as he goes
into a shopping mall to check out potential victims:

> *Noon was approaching and waves of heat rose from the cars in
> the lot. Barton was sensitive to heat. The other kids had called
> him 'Leaky', he sweated so much. That and 'Fat Royal'.*
>
> *That was a long time ago – longer than it felt. But mentally
> Barton was never far from his own childhood. He kept going
> over things. People who remembered childhood fondly were
> lucky; they were the ones who had put the pain to rest.*
>
> *Crossing the pavement he bowed his head against the sun and
> was grateful to push through the doors into the air
> conditioning. In the old days department stores had smelled
> like malls did now… The smell always took him back to the
> days when his gang – well, not really <u>his</u>, but the gang he was
> in – used to ride bikes down to Woolworth's on Main and
> Mariposa where they had a comic book rack and cap guns
> and toy soldiers and a lunch counter where you could get a
> hamburger and large Cherry Coke for seventy-five cents. He
> wasn't really in the gang, of course, but he rode with them. Or
> rather, he took the same route. The guys would all sit at the
> counter; he would be in a booth nearby.*

The picture the author paints here of Barton is one of childhood
exclusion. Unless we are incredibly lucky, we have all experienced
the feeling of being an outsider. We may have moved to a new
area, attended a new school, or joined a club where everyone else
knew each other. Even if only temporary, that feeling of not
belonging will have stuck with us to the extent that we know – on
one level – how Barton might feel.

But Barton was an ugly child, too, and while we may be repulsed by his sweaty appearance, we also know how important acceptance of one's appearance is for self-esteem. In ordinary circumstances, we'd feel sympathy for Barton. Barton's actions make that impossible. However, these viewpoint glimpses into his background ensure that he's no cardboard monster. He is real.

W. H. Auden wrote that: *Those to whom evil is done do evil in return.* In Barton's case, his psychopathic behaviour is motivated by a damaging and desperate need that has never been satisfied. To explore that need, the author did what those Delta flight attendants do every day. He 'reframed' the story from Barton's perspective.

All characters become more substantial when the author knows something of their emotional baggage. To give you practice in reframing, try the following exercise. In writing classes, I often ask students to pair up for the second part. If you have a friend handy, you might want to try this. However, both ways work well.

THE EXERCISE

Make a list of situations in which you've felt irritated, angry or hurt by someone. Include a mix of situations, serious ones as well as petty ones. Choose one situation to explore in role play.

If you're working with a friend, s/he will now play 'you', while you role-play the instigator of your anger or hurt. For example, suppose one of your situations involves a rude work colleague. Your friend presents your grievance and your task is to role-play the colleague, defending yourself as best you can. To do this, you mentally step into the other person's shoes. Don't think of this as trying to get at the 'true' situation. The whole point of this exercise is to show how situations change when we're obliged to take the other side. It works because studies suggest that role — or what we perceive as our role — has a huge influence on our behaviour. In one well-known experiment, for example, ordinary people who role-played prisoners actually began to feel disempowered. By contrast, those who role-played prison guards experienced feelings of empowerment.

If you're working on your own, use the Delta airlines technique of making up a story to explain the behaviour. You'll still step into the antagonist's shoes, but instead of defending yourself in a face-to-face confrontation, write the story down. Feel free to bring in as much background detail as you like.

34

Say 'No' to Crocodile Tears

'Nonfiction conveys information. Fiction evokes emotion,' said Sol Stein to an audience of writers in Barnes and Noble's bookstore in Union Square, New York. 'Memorise that,' he said. 'Put it on a slip of paper and tape it to your computer until it's permanently engraved in your memory.'

Why is emotion so important? Because it's the 'glue' that pulls all the other disparate elements together. When readers pick up a novel, they're looking for something that matches their mood. Genre fiction is even categorised by the feelings it's designed to provoke. If we want to be frightened, we head for the horror section. If we're in the mood for love, we check out romance. If we want excitement without having to worry *too* much about headless horsemen attacking us in our sleep, we choose cosy crime. And if we're undecided, we riffle through dust jackets, until we find one that 'looks' good.

For many new writers, however, getting emotion onto the pages is a touch problematic. 'I don't understand why no one found my piece moving,' a student recently complained. 'I had a lump in my throat as I wrote it.' I believed her. Unfortunately, emotion is not a cheese sandwich. The more we struggle to describe it, the less the reader is involved. Often the best we can do is to trot out our own physical symptoms – the pounding heart, the sweaty palms, the butterflies in the stomach. The feeling itself remains tantalisingly elusive.

There's a reason for this. Emotions are experienced in an area of the brain that is dumb. This area is deep in the right hemisphere of the brain, whereas our language centres are in the left. You may have experienced this hemispherical difference when listening to music. As Anthony Storr reports in his fascinating book, *Music and Mind*, certain types of orchestral music have been shown to arouse strong emotion, yet other than naming the emotion – sadness, joy, wistfulness, and so on – listeners are unable to verbalise what they feel. This is because music is mainly scanned and processed by the right hemisphere. In fact, music can still affect a listener emotionally when the left hemisphere has been sedated, or damaged. Studies show that left-brain damaged composers can still compose and even teach music, despite losing their ability to speak. By contrast, damage to the right hemisphere inhibits all sorts of emotion-related abilities, including singing, understanding of metaphor and recognition of facial expression.

For writers, therefore, the best way of getting emotion or mood across to the reader is to concentrate not on feeling itself but on the context. In other words, if you want to convey fear, you show the situation that gave rise to the fear. That way, readers will have first-hand knowledge instead of second-hand description. To help you along with this, start experimenting with what T. S. Eliot called 'objective correlatives':

> *The only way of expressing emotion in the form of art is by finding an 'objective correlative'; in other words, a set of objects, a situation, a chain of events which shall be the formula for that particular emotion; such that when the external facts, which must terminate in sensory experience, are given, the emotion is immediately evoked.*
> (quoted in J. A. Cuddon's *Dictionary of Literary Terms*, p. 647)

Objective correlatives act as metaphors for mood or emotion, and like other metaphors their appeal is not to logic but to feeling. For example, the metaphorical comment that 'I have measured out my life in coffee spoons' in Eliot's *The Love Song of J Arthur Prufrock*, does more to capture Prufrock's sense of a life wasted on trifling domesticity than pages of emotive descriptive detail. You can use these correlatives singly, or – as Eliot suggests – blend them together into a formula or 'set' of symbols that work together. For example, in the old Hammer horror films, gothic mansions, swirling mist, moonlight, and hooting owls were an artistic mix of spine-chilling elements. When people watched these films, nobody told them to feel scared. They felt scared because the objects were already associated with the uncanny.

OK, it may be corny, but we still read and enjoy books like Daphne du Maurier's *Rebecca,* Bram Stoker's *Dracula,* and Susan Hill's *The Woman in Black,* all of which draw on objective correlatives from the gothic tradition.

When establishing objective correlatives, however, you can invent your own associations. In *You're Ugly, Too,* originally published in the prestigious *New Yorker* magazine, Lorrie Moore uses the situation of going to the cinema as an objective correlative. Zoe Hendricks, an unmarried history professor, is at the movies on her own. Having bought some strands of red liquorice to tug and chew, she sits to one side and waits for the lights to go down. When they do:

> *... she reached inside her purse for her glasses. They were in a Baggie. Her Kleenex was also in a Baggie. So were her pen and her aspirin and her mints. Everything was in Baggies. This was what she'd become: a woman alone at the movies with everything in a Baggie.*

Because cinema-going – buying sweets, choosing your seat and so on – is normally associated with companionship, this situation highlights both the character's aloneness and the pathos of her realisation. Any number of other objective correlatives might have worked just as well.

Sometimes, you can establish objective correlatives as an emotional 'thread' to be pulled at various points in the story. For example, if an elderly man takes pride in cleaning his lawnmower and other garden tools after working in his garden, you could use these objects to symbolise the man's independence. Later, if the man's independence is threatened, the dusty lawnmower and rusting tools will help to heighten your emotional content.

What you have done here is to create your own recurring motif, a technique much favoured by Ernest Hemingway. In *A Farewell to Arms,* rain is just one of many objective correlatives Hemingway sets up as a metaphor for death. As those of you who have read the book will know, this is a tragic First World War romance which ends with Frederick's lover, Catherine, giving birth to a dead baby boy. Frederick then stays with Catherine in her hospital room until she, too, dies. Finally, he tells the nurses to leave:

> *But after I had got them out and shut the door and turned off the light it wasn't any good. It was like saying goodbye to a statue. After a while I went out and left the hospital and walked back to the hotel in the rain.*

Taken out of context, this may not seem particularly moving. It's raining – so what? However, to readers who have stayed the course, the rain has become a potent symbol of human mortality.

Just as rain can fall at any time on anyone, so death can happen to anyone at any time. Nor have we the power to control rain, which, in the book, tends to fall when characters are in situations of danger or uncertainty, such as saying goodbye when boarding a train, or narrowly avoiding death. Catherine herself is afraid of the rain. As a nurse during the war, she has had more experience of death than Frederick, who begins by liking the rain but eventually comes to experience it as she does.

Without this preparation, the final words wouldn't have the power to affect us. As it is, they allow Hemingway to create emotional impact while keeping Frederick's physical feelings to a minimum. When he says, 'It was like saying goodbye to a statue', readers expect it to be raining, and rain is as much a part of our emotion as of his.

THE EXERCISE

Here are some objects and elements ripe for correlation. Pick one and use in a five-minute paragraph designed to reveal mood, feelings or emotion. You might note that some of these objects already have associations. Feel free to use these as they stand, or, like Lorrie Moore, challenge the established meaning to forge new ones. By all means add other objects to create a compound effect. The aim here is to avoid making explicit reference to mood. Let it emerge through the specific object or combination of objects.

a black crow

mirror

falling leaves

china tea set

pot plant

sports car

crowded train

cashpoint machine

new haircut

bottle of whiskey

sunshine

Christmas tree

the sea

piano

wallpaper with a pattern of
  trellis and vines

35

Daisy Chain Stories

'The foot bone's connected to the ankle bone, the ankle bone's connected to the leg bone, the leg bone's connected to the knee bone ...'

We may not remember all the words, but everyone knows the song, an old African-American spiritual based on a vision in Ezekiel. According to the story, the prophet Ezekiel went out into the desert, found a heap of dry bones and brought them to life by talking to them. Fiction writers may not be prophets, but there are certainly a couple of messages in there for us.

First, if you want to create something, start looking for connections, things which don't mean much on their own but which you can link together into a satisfying whole. Second, stories are about people. When we talk about story 'skeletons', we're usually thinking of plot, with the bones representing significant events throughout the narrative. Let's look at this another way. Instead of the bones representing events, what would happen if we thought of them as characters whose connections we can explore?

For example, we might have Anna connected to Beatrice, Beatrice connected to Christopher, Christopher connected to Debbie, and so on. If we then connect the last character in this series – let's call him Kieran – back to Anna, we have the makings of a daisy chain story. This circular structure is one that has fascinated many writers, who have used it to explore particular themes. One of the most famous is Arthur Schnitzler's play *La Ronde,* a series of sexual encounters which was considered too obscene to be performed in public when Schnitzler wrote it in 1900. That changed in 1950 when Max Ophuls adapted it for film. More recently, David Hare rewrote it as *The Blue Room* for the London stage.

The Blue Room is a fascinating play containing ten characters, five women and five men. It begins with a meeting between 'The girl' and 'The cab driver'. When the scene ends, the cab driver moves on to the next character in line, 'The au pair'. At the end of that scene, the au pair connects with 'The student', and so on. Eventually, the last character, 'The aristocrat' meets up with 'The girl'.

Although the focus here is sexual mores, daisy chain stories can explore any theme. The film *Love Actually,* while still containing sex, is – as its title suggests – more concerned with love. Within this overall remit, its ten separate but intertwining stories explore a different idea or subsidiary theme. For Jamie (Colin Firth) and Aurelia (Lucia Moniz), the theme is 'love as a second language'. Aurelia is Portuguese and can't speak English, whereas Jamie is English and can't speak Portuguese. For David (Hugh Grant) and Natalie (Martine McCutcheon), it's 'love and politics'. David is prime minister and Natalie's the tea girl. For the other eight, check out the official website at *www.loveactually.com* – or watch the film.

You can even use this daisy chain model to provide structure and continuity in a short story. Normally, short stories work best with just one viewpoint character, but *Hope Springs Eternal* by

Elizabeth Candlish contains seven. It begins with an elderly woman, Maisie MacFarlane, hoping that someone will come and visit her. As she perches herself by her sitting room window:

> *She couldn't remember the last time there had been an unexpected visitor, but never mind, there was always the chance. Anyway, she liked to see people go by; it made the day more interesting. And sure enough, there was somebody already, Mrs Rumbold from number 69, with her shopping trolley too – must be expecting her son at the weekend.*

But Mrs Rumbold doesn't call on Maisie. Nor do we, the readers, continue to share her thoughts. Instead, the writer switches to Mrs Rumbold who is busy wondering whether her son Derek will be coming to see her on Sunday, or not. The story continues, with each new character picking up the metaphorical baton and running to the next. Finally, the last person in the circle loops back to Maisie. This story, like other circular narratives, is a series of tightly-woven cameos, linked by theme – the characters' hopes and dreams.

THE EXERCISE

◆ Choose seven character names. If you've done Exercise 12, The Name of the Game, you'll have a ready supply of these. If you haven't, take five minutes to do that exercise, and then return here.

◆ Pick two of the characters and write a five-minute scene, from one point of view, focusing on a disagreement. Don't think too hard about this. Just let it happen.

Congratulations. You have the start of a circular story. For your next five minutes, pick up the second character from your first scene and write another scene from their point of view. What effect did the disagreement have on them? What are they thinking now? Where are they going? Who else might be affected? Either include the third character, or mention him or her towards the end. And so on.

When you've finished, you may not have a great daisy chain story, but what you will have is seven viable characters whose intertwining lives may just the catalyst you need to get you going on that full-length novel.

36

The Café of Life

If you watch television soap operas, you'll have noticed that one thing they all have in common is unity of place, meaning that the significant action occurs in a single familiar setting. In Britain, this successful format began in 1960, with *Coronation Street,* in which all the main characters live on the same gloomy street in a northern town called Weatherfield and exchange their stories in the same local pub. Now, we have *EastEnders, Brookfield,* and *Emmerdale,* whose titles define that scenic unity.

What the writers have created here is a focus or backdrop for a whole community of stories. There's no need for characters to justify their appearance. Their presence in the community is justification in itself. But you don't need to be writing a soap opera to reap the benefits of this format. For example, in *Quentins,* Maeve Binchy chooses a Dublin restaurant as her backdrop. The publicity blurb explains:

> *Every table at Quentins restaurant has a thousand stories to tell: tales of love, betrayal and revenge. There has been hope and despair sitting in the chairs. The staff who come and go have stories of their own, and the restaurant itself has had times when it looked set fair for success and others when it seemed as if it must close in failure.*

The character Binchy uses to bring these disparate tales together is documentary film-maker Ella Brady, who visited Quentins for the first time as a child. Now grown up, Ella wants to use the restaurant's history to capture the spirit of Dublin from the 1970s to the present day. She also has her own story to tell and this acts as a unifying voice throughout the book.

Another writer who's used this format with great success is Arthur Hailey whose two best-known novels, *Hotel* and *Airport* – both written in the 1960s – became feature films. In *Hotel,* we have a cast of characters whose loves and lives converge at the luxurious St Gregory Hotel in New Orleans. For *Airport,* another cast of characters find their fates intertwined at Lincoln International Airport outside Chicago.

If you'd like to have a go at using this format, take a fresh look at your favourite café. Try the following exercise.

THE EXERCISE

Choose a cafe to visit. It could be a smart city coffee shop, a greasy spoon, or a small-town 'copper kettle', serving tea and home-made cake. Order a cup of coffee and sit down in a place where you can observe the other customers. For me, my local Starbucks in the evening is brilliant for this because it's next to Sainsbury's. If I sit in the window, I can watch everyone walk by. And inside, because there's always noise – expresso machines hissing and orders being sent down the line to the barrista – people don't seem to realise how their voices carry. Confidences are exchanged, secrets told: 'Now, John, keep this under your hat, I haven't even told Peter yet ...' is a typical example.

As you sit there, let the different people suggest themselves to you. Some will catch your interest, some will not. When you're ready, spend your five minutes jotting down a few brief details about each potential character, so that you can recall them later.

If questions occur to you, jot those down as well. For example, who is the elderly bearded man, wearing Dunlop Green Flash tennis shoes, who comes in every night for a small expresso? Is he a retired intellectual? What is his story?

It's In the Bag

*She was carrying an enormous black leather bag, capacious
and heavy, and full of unnecessary things … a number of
crumpled tissues, some pink, some white, a spray bottle of
'Wild Musk' cologne … a pair of nail scissors, a pair of nail
clippers, a London tube pass, a British Telecom phone card,
an address book, a mascara wand in a shade called 'After-
midnight blue' … a postcard from a friend on holiday in
Brittany, a calculator, a paperback of Vasari's* Lives of the
Artists *… three-quarters of a bar of milk chocolate …*

Ruth Rendell, *A Pair of Yellow Lilies*

Why catalogue the contents of a woman's handbag? A handbag is
the ultimate private space and that, for a writer, is juicy territory.
Nathalie Lecroc is a French artist who paints watercolour
'portraits' of the contents of people's handbags. If it's in there,
she paints it, including, on one occasion, a limp old lettuce leaf.
'The owner was incredibly embarrassed that I painted it,' says
Lecroc.

According to Lecroc, many people find the painting an emotional
experience, partly because Lecroc includes a detailed analysis of
what she believes the contents say about their owner. 'It's
incredible what you can say about people after just two or three
hours with their bags,' she told *American Vogue*. 'It's the same
kind of insight you get when you sit with somebody at dinner.'
One client's bag, for example, contained a little gadget for

hooking on the edge of a table so its owner could hang her bag from that, rather than placing her precious belongings on the floor. I bet *she* didn't have lettuce lurking among her lipsticks.

The idea for exploring character by rummaging in people's personal belongings first came to Lecroc when she found a wallet on the Paris street where she lives. She discovered that its owner was a soldier and became fascinated by the power of small everyday objects to reveal personality. Writers, too, can use this method for creating characters. Before doing the following exercise, however, you might like to tip out the contents of your own bag and think what they might reveal about you. When I did this, I was surprised to find how many pens I was carrying around – a sign, perhaps of my obsessive-compulsive need to be able to make notes.

EXERCISE

Imagine you've found someone's bag, briefcase, purse, or other smallish container. You don't know who its owner is but you decide to find out by being nosey. You open the bag and pull out the contents. Without thinking too hard, list at least six items. Don't just go for the obvious mobile phone and tissues, although you can of course include these, too.

Now, write a short character sketch, based on the items you've discovered.

The Taste of Success

A creamy blur of succulent blue sound smells like week-old
strawberries dropped onto a tin sieve as mother approaches in
a halo of colour, chatter and a perfume like thick golden
butterscotch.

Diane Ackerman, *A Natural History of the Senses*

According to Diane Ackerman, this is how newborn babies
perceive their world, intermingling waves of sight, sound, touch,
taste, and smell. When adults experience their world like this, we
call them synaesthetes, people for whom a stimulus to one sense
produces sensations in another. A synaesthete may 'hear' colours,
'see' sounds as colours, or 'taste' tactile sensations. For example,
one man interviewed on the BBC's *Horizon* programme,
experienced names as tastes. For him, Derek 'tasted' of earwax.

The UK Synaesthesia Association suggests that one in 2,000 of us
is a synaesthete, and it appears to be more common among
creative people, including painters, writers and musicians. The
composer, Rimsky-Korsakov, was reputed to be a synaesthete in
that he associated colours with music as he wrote. C major was
white, whereas A major was rose.

However, latest research suggests that we all have some capacity
for synaesthesia without even being aware of it. If someone
describes the taste of a particular cheese as 'sharp', for example,
you know what they mean, even though 'sharp' is not a taste. You

know what a 'loud pink' dress is, even though pink is not a sound.
Similarly, we're all familiar with synaesthesia as a poetic device in
metaphorical writing. 'Annihilating all that's made, To a green
thought in a green shade', wrote Andrew Marvell in *The Garden*.
Similarly, Nick Carraway, the narrator of F. Scott Fitzgerald's *The
Great Gatsby*, writes of the 'yellow cocktail music' that plays at
Gatsby's parties.

According to cognitive psychologists Vilayanur Ramachandran
and Edward M. Hubbard, synaesthesia, creativity, and use of
metaphor may all have a similar neural basis, which helps to
explain the increased occurrence of synaesthesia among painters,
poets and novelists. Quoting a metaphorical line from
Shakespeare as an example – 'It is the east and Juliet is the sun' –
they suggest that:

> *It is as if their brains are set up to make links between
> seemingly unrelated domains – such as the sun and a beautiful
> young woman. In other words, just as synaesthesia involves
> making arbitrary links between seemingly unrelated perceptual
> entities such as colours and numbers, metaphor involves
> making links between seemingly unrelated conceptual realms.*
>
> Ramachandran, V. S. and Hubbard, E. (2003),
> 'Hearing Colors, Tasting Shapes', *Scientific American*,
> Vol 288, Issue 5 (May 2003), pp. 42–49

If this is true, then experimenting with synaesthetic images may
not only help you to create more exciting metaphors but may also
help you to be more creative, and that can't be bad. You don't
have to be a synaesthete to do this. In *Mondays are Red,* Nicola
Morgan made her main character a synaesthete because she had
always been fascinated by the sensory potential of synaesthesia: 'I

wanted to open readers' minds to the endless possibilities of our wonderful language.' Written in the first person, the novel tells the story of Luke, a teenager who wakes up from a coma to discover he has 'a kaleidoscope' in his head:

> *Mondays are red. Sadness has an empty blue smell. And*
> *music can taste of anything from banana puree to bat's pee.*

In Luke's new world, violin music sounds like lemons, a smile is orange-scented, and strawberry music flows from the touch of his mother's fingers. Try the following exercise.

THE EXERCISE

Use synaesthesia in a short scene to give your reader a sensory experience of what you're trying to convey. First, get your scene into your head. Then start thinking of aspects of the scene in terms of other senses. For example, flowing water normally makes a sound, but you might want to describe it in terms of things that have a taste. Perhaps a fountain might sound like splinters of glacier mints, or a slow-moving river might be like thick honey. Similarly, think of the sound of people's voices. To me, for example, the actor Jodie Foster's voice is like strands of black liquorice, while Clint Eastwood has a pleasant tang of disinfectant.

Try, too, experimenting with the smell of emotions. For example, in real life we often talk about the smell of fear, but what is the smell? Is it like stale cabbage or something else? Does it have a colour? You choose. For everything you want to describe, run through all the senses and see what comes up. Remember, this is not something you do every day so it may feel a bit strange at first.

Choice and Consequence –
Two Magic Ingredients

In Robert Frost's famous poem, *The Road not Taken,* a traveller comes to two roads in a yellow wood and can't decide which one to take. Eventually, he selects the path whose grass is longer, the one 'less travelled', as Frost puts it. Frost's motivation for writing the poem came from his own experience of visiting a friend, Edward Thomas, who lived in Gloucestershire. Thomas, anxious to show Frost the best of the British countryside, would always choose a route that enabled him to point out a rare plant or a good view. Later, he would always regret his choice and start to sigh over what he might have been able to show Frost on the other path.

Even if we've never been on a country walk in our lives, we can all identify with Thomas's mixed feelings. Metaphorically, that grassy path could symbolise anything from a different job to a new relationship. Should we play safe and stick with what we know? Or should we take a chance? Life is a series of choices. Some are easy, some are hard. However, as Alan Ayckbourn showed so beautifully in *Intimate Exchanges,* a play which starts with a woman trying to decide whether to have her first cigarette of the day before 6 o'clock, all choices have consequences – even though the consequences may not immediately be apparent.

Any fiction writer who takes this simple principle of choice and consequence to heart has a perfect model that will work for all stories. In fact, without choice and consequence, there is no story. That holds true for both popular and literary fiction.

A writing class student recently challenged me on this, citing *Captain Corelli's Mandolin* by Louis de Bernières. In fact, the choice and consequence dynamic is the author's main technique for introducing his rich cast of Second World War characters. In the beginning chapters, for example:

1. Dr Iannis has to decide on the best way to remove a dried pea from an old man's ear, a pea that has been so long in situ as to acquire a *hard brown cankerous coating of wax*.

2. Prime Minister Metaxas has to decide what to do about his daughter Lulu, whose wild behaviour at parties is becoming an embarrassment.

3. Meanwhile, Father Arsenios, trapped by duty in his church confessional, must decide what to do about his full bladder.

The function of each dilemma for the readers is two-fold. First, it gives the characters an immediate goal, and that's important if you don't want a static story. Second, it encourages the readers to think what they would do under similar circumstances. When readers engage with a story in this way, they take the first step towards making the story their own. For this reason, it's far better to start a story with a character desperate for the loo – a problem with which everyone can identify – than a complex situation that has no meaning outside the story. Readers don't care about a story until they can see themselves and their own lives reflected in the character's dilemma.

THE EXERCISE

To incorporate choice and consequence in your fiction, start thinking of your story in terms of a tree structure. In the above diagram, a character's journey through the plot starts at the trunk and moves upwards. The first branch equates with Robert Frost's fork in the road, at which alternative possibilities exist. Here, the character has to decide which way to go, or what decision to make.

Note that you can't give a character a choice without first creating a situation that requires a decision. Yes, I know this is obvious to some of you, but beginners' stories often fail for this very reason. By all means, think of your own situation or try this one for size:

Your character is in bed, when the front door bell rings. This is the first decision point. Does your character stay in bed, or does s/he get up to answer the door?

As I hope you can see, it's your character's choice that drives the story forward. What are the consequences of his or her decision? What happens next along the pathway s/he's chosen? This may be an external event – Thomas Hardy was fond of using storms to give his characters something to think about — or it could be something directly related to the character's previous choice. Either way, the character moves though the story, actualising one particular pathway over another.

In your five-minute writing slot, jot down as many decision points you can until you run out of time. Don't worry about an ending, or even writing a good story. The purpose of this exercise is simply to get you using choice and consequence. At some point, in much the same way as a literal pathway might lead to a dead end, you may find that the story is going nowhere. If this happens, simply go back and have your character actualise a different path.

What Do You Care About?

In Patricia MacLachlan's *All the Places to Love,* baby Eli's grandmother wraps him in a blanket made from the wool of her own sheep and holds him up to the window so that:

What I heard first was the wind.
What I saw first was all the places to love:
The valley,
The river falling down over rocks,
The hilltop where the blueberries grew.

Written in the voice of a child who lives on a farm, *All the Places to Love* celebrates the natural world and strong family ties. Its author, Patricia MacLachlan, was born on the American prairie, and claims to still carry a small bag of prairie soil around with her to remind her of the place she knew first. 'I think all my books are about family,' she says. 'Families fascinate me, how they work or don't work; how the members affect each other.'

When writers write about the things that matter to them, it shows. As novelist John Gardner said: 'A writer's material is what he cares about.' This doesn't mean we all have to write about nature and happy families. Lawyer Andrew Vachss became a novelist because he cares about juvenile delinquency. His tough crime novels champion the rights of abused children, and are, he believes, a much better way of publicising his message than 'pious rhetoric' in the courts.

By contrast, Lynne Truss cares passionately about punctuation – which is perhaps why *Eats, Shoots and Leaves* became a best-seller. Nigella Lawson loves food, which may explain why we devour her books. Kevin Crossley-Holland is passionate about the medieval imagination, which fuels his retelling of classical stories like the Arthurian legend. And so on. What do you care about? Try the following exercise.

EXERCISE

Make a list of things that you care about. Include anything that you love, and anything that matters to you, particularly if it's something about which you feel passionate. Or if you can't identify your passions, start with what you like:

> I like: salad, cinnamon, cheese, pimento, marzipan, the smell of new-cut hay, roses, peonies, lavender, champagne, loosely held political convictions, Glenn Gould, too-cold beer, flat pillows, toast, Havana cigars, Handel, slow walks, pears, white peaches, cherries, colours, watches, all kinds of writing pens, desserts, unrefined salt, realistic novels...
>
> Roland Barthes, *Roland Barthes*

A variation on this exercise is to list what you don't like, which, in Barthes' case, includes women in slacks, geraniums, animated cartoons, telephoning, fidelity, and evenings with people he doesn't know.

Beautiful Words

What is the most beautiful word in the English language? Chocolate? Try again. According to a survey run by the British Council, the number one word is mother, closely followed by passion and smile (read the complete list of 70 beautiful words on the British Council's website: *www.britishcouncil.org/home-70-beautiful-words.htm*). What is it about these words that gets people going? Given that the survey included 40,000 voters in 46 countries, it would seem like there's something universal going on here. Tap your own associations in the following exercise.

mother	destiny	sunshine	grace
passion	freedom	sweetheart	rainbow
smile	liberty	gorgeous	fantastic
love	tranquillity	cherish	blossom
eternity	peace	enthusiasm	hope

Not-So-Beautiful Words

What makes a word ugly? According to Ross Eckler, editor of *Word Ways,* a journal of recreational linguistics, ugly words seem more likely than others to contain several different hard consonants. Using this criterion, clodhopper, buttock, and toilet are not going to win any beauty contests. I wonder, though, if it doesn't also have something to do with their meaning. Some words may sound ugly but others just have ugly connotations, depending on individual associations. An old poll by the National Association of Teachers of Speech, for example, revealed their ten worst-sounding words to be: cacophony, crunch, flatulent, gripe, jazz, phlegmatic, plump, plutocrat, sap and treachery. Speaking personally, cacophony seems a relatively inoffensive word, but I guess if you're a teacher trying to control an unruly bunch of children, you might have other ideas. Similarly, I don't like the word 'sycamore' because there was one on my route to school and I frequently did feel physically sick as I walked under it.

THE EXERCISE

Make your own list of ugly words or words that you dislike for their looks, sound or associations.

Plunge-in Beginnings

*Renowned curator Jacques Sauniere staggered though the
vaulted archway of the museum's Grand Gallery. He lunged
for the nearest painting he could see, a Caravaggio. Grabbing
the gilded frame, the seventy-six-year-old man heaved the
masterpiece toward himself until it tore from the wall and
Sauniere collapsed backward in a heap beneath the canvas.*

*As he had anticipated, a thundering iron gate fell nearby,
barricading the entrance to the suite. The parquet floor shook.
Far off, an alarm began to ring.*

Dan Brown, *The Da Vinci Code*

Heady stuff, huh? While the *Da Vinci Code* remained in the *New
York Times* Best Seller list for an impressive two years, Dan
Brown's other books, *Angels and Demons*, *Digital Fortress*, and
Deception Point are all best-sellers, too. By anyone's definition,
Brown is a fantastically successful blockbuster writer who really
knows how to the keep his readers turning the pages. His novels
all open with something going on. In the above extract, Jacques
Sauniere deliberately sets off the museum's alarm system as a
desperate attempt to escape from his killer. Few readers could
resist turning the page to see if he succeeds.

Two of Dan Brown's other books also begin with characters
about to die. The rationale here is obvious. If a technique works,
stick with it.

But you don't have to adopt the same situation to use the technique. On his official website, Brown cites Sidney Sheldon as one of the biggest influences on his early writing career. In 1994, while on holiday in Tahiti, he found an old copy of Sidney Sheldon's *Doomsday Conspiracy* on the beach: 'I read the first page ... and then the next ... and then the next ...' Keen readers will notice many similarities between the two writers' styles. Sheldon writes plunge-in beginnings. He also often repeats a gripping motif, such as characters waking from dreams or nightmares. Take, for example, the start of *Memories of Midnight*:

> *She woke up screaming every night and it was always the same dream. She was in the middle of a lake in a fierce storm and a man and a woman were forcing her head under the waters, drowning her.*

Another motif, perhaps a shade less dramatic but no less engaging is the idea of being followed. Take *Morning, Noon and Night*:

> *Dmitri asked 'Do you know we're being followed, Mr Stanford?'*
> *'Yes.' He had been aware of them for the past twenty-four hours.*

Or *Tell Me Your Dreams*:

> *Someone was following her. She had read about stalkers, but they belonged in a different, violent world.*

What all these beginnings have in common is their ability to plunge the readers into the story world. They work because (a) they present a situation with which we all can identify, and (b) they get us asking questions. Of course, you *can* start your story with a moody description of a sunset, but readers have more motivation for staying with you if you give them the feeling that the ride is already moving. 'Jump on,' these beginnings say, 'and all will be revealed.' It's not that difficult. Try this technique for yourself with the following exercise.

THE EXERCISE

Choose one of the following scenarios to use as a beginning. Freewrite for five minutes. Don't think about what you're writing. Just see where it leads.

- Write about a character who is being followed.

- Write about a character who is following someone. Remember, not all followers are sinister.

- Write about a character being awoken from a dream or nightmare. What awakens them? Phone call? Children jumping on top of them? Dog licking their face? Use your imagination.

- Write about a character receiving a letter that (in some way) changes their life.

- Write about a character who is driving along searching for something or someone.

- Write about a character who has just received some unpleasant news.

44

Writing with Titles

The first words readers see when they pick a story or a novel are those in the title. A strong title immediately evokes an emotional reaction. Consider *Mystic River* by Dennis Lehane, *I Capture the Castle* by Dodie Smith, or *Cold Mountain* by Charles Frazier. Hardly surprising then that authors often agonise over several different titles before coming up with the one that appears on the cover. Margaret Mitchell's original title for *Gone with the Wind* was *Pansy*, named after the heroine who later became Scarlett. Then someone suggested *Tomorrow is another Day,* but there were already 16 other books of that name. Mitchell's final choice was a line from a poem by Ernest Dowson which she liked because 'it had the far away, faintly sad sound I wanted.'

By contrast, James Patterson favours a nursery rhyme theme for his novels featuring Washington cop Alex Cross. The first – *Along Came a Spider* – was originally called *Remember Maggie Rose,* but Cross and his editor thought that nursery rhymes would make it easier for readers to remember his books.

Other writers are inspired by songs. *We'll Meet Again* was an old wartime number sung by Vera Lynn until Mary Higgins Clark turned it into a thriller. She has also used a hymn – *Silent Night* – for a Christmas suspense story.

For some writers, a working title is itself the first step in writing. In an interview with *Saga Magazine,* Angela Huth explained how she was looking out at the lawn one evening and the daisies were all closed. Immediately she thought 'When the daisies close' would be a good title. Next day, the BBC rang, asking for a story on the theme of old age. Huth thought of the daisy title and wrote a story about an ageing couple whose children wanted them to move into a retirement bungalow.

Experimenting with titles is one great way to flex your writing muscle when you're short of time. Try the following exercise when you're stuck in a queue or waiting for the traffic lights to change.

Compile a list of titles for some new stories. You might concentrate on a particular genre such as romance, horror, sci-fi, or you might choose a theme. You don't have to develop any of these into actual stories. However, given that titles can be highly evocative; don't be surprised if you find yourself inspired.

If you get stuck, here are some themed triggers, including examples:

'Number' titles. (*The Three Little Pigs, The Famous Five, The Four Horsemen of the Apocalypse.*)

'Person's name' titles. (*The Talented Mr Ripley, Smiley's People, Bridget Jones' Diary.*)

'Place name' titles. (*Wuthering Heights, Brighton Rock, A Town Like Alice.*)

'Colour' titles. (*Black Beauty, The Girl with Green Eyes, The Colour Purple.*)

Alliterative titles. (*The Clan of the Cave Bear, Pride and Prejudice, The Shell Seekers.*)

'Food' titles. (*Chocolat, An Ice Cream War, Oranges are not the only Fruit.*)

'Drink' titles. (*Cider with Rosie, Blackberry Wine, The Long Dark Tea Time of the Soul.*)

Amusing titles. (*Parsley, Sage, Rosemary and Crime, Between a Wok and a Hard Place, The Crepes of Wrath.* (These three titles are from Tamar Myers' Pennsylvania Dutch mysteries. The setting is an inn in the fictional town of Hernia.)

Visual Dialogue

Visual dialogue? Surely that's a mistake – unless your characters are using sign language? Well no, it isn't a mistake. As Dianne Doubtfire points out in *Creative Writing,* novices often have their characters speaking in a vacuum, which means that there are no visual clues to anchor the reader in the physical setting. As an example, Doubtfire cites the student who began a dialogue exchange between two businessmen in a car:

It was dramatic and well edited but it failed because there was no background for their confrontation … After a page or two we forgot they were in a car and when at last they got out of it we were flabbergasted.

One way to fix this is to include some scenic detail. Another rather more sophisticated way is to integrate the dialogue with some kind of action. In other words, give the characters something to do. When dialogue, action and setting work together, you have a dynamic mix that really draws the reader into the story. The simplest example of this is the archetypal restaurant, bar, or cafe scene:

A waiter appeared bearing bread and rosemary-scented olive oil. He arranged the items on the table and departed. Zoe tore off a large chunk of bread and plunged it into the olive oil. She paused just long enough to sprinkle a little salt on the oil-saturated bread, and then she took a very large bite. 'Are you sure you're all right?' Arcadia remained unconvinced.

'No offense, but you look somewhat the worse for wear?'

'I'm fine,' Zoe said around the mouthful of dense, chewy bread. 'The problem is: what do I do now?'

Jayne Ann Krentz, *Light in Shadow*

There's no real reason why this conversation can't take place over the telephone. And do we really need to know Zoe's taste in bread? Probably not. The purpose here is to keep the story visual, both on a character level and a scenic level. As a technique, it works, which is the reason most novels and films usually include a scene where characters discuss things over a meal. In the days before smoking became socially unacceptable, there was the cigarette lighting ritual, too. Many a private eye has kept the readers in tow with a packet of Camels, or a pipe needing constant attention to stop it going out.

Nowadays, in our health-conscious society, such characters are probably more likely to exchange confidences as they exercise in a gym, but there are plenty of alternatives, and it's worth having a stockpile of ways to keep your characters' hands busy. For example, could one of your characters have an interesting or unusual job? It doesn't have to be the main character. In Sue Grafton's *A is for Alibi*, private eye Kinsey Millhone interviews a groomer in a dog's beauty parlour. She gets answers to her questions while a poodle called Wuffles is combed and clipped.

Almost any job can sound fascinating when translated into action. It doesn't need to be anything strenuous. I remember watching a television play in which a woman stood at a kitchen table, making sage and onion stuffing. I can still see her cutting up the onions as she talked. To get ideas, watch some films. You'll find that dialogue exchanges are rarely static.

THE EXERCISE

Start a list of activities a character or characters might be doing as they talk. To get you going, here are some ideas:

moving furniture around	sanding a floor
fencing	cleaning (anything)
playing cards	ironing clothes
fishing	weeding the garden

Once you've got a list, pick one activity and write a dialogue exchange, remembering to integrate your character's dialogue with the action.

You *Can* Write a Story in Five Minutes

I know you're shaking your head, but – trust me – you can. It won't be a long story and it probably won't be a great one, either, but you can do it. The secret lies in knowing what a story is at its most basic, what minimal condition is necessary for a story to exist. With this element in place, you can write a 'story' in a very few words. Without it, you will never create a satisfying story, no matter how much you write.

How do I know this? Because narratologists have spent years studying different varieties of story in both oral and written language with the aim of finding a common minimal dynamic. Consider the following three examples. See if you can identify which, if any, contains that dynamic.

♦ A man leapt from his car to collar three thieves stealing from a church gift shop in Rochester, Kent – and was given a parking ticket as he waited for the police.

♦ An uninvited guest has been discovered in hundreds of wedding photos in the New Zealand town of Dunedin. Couples have only just noticed that the same woman appears at the edge of nearly all the town's Catholic weddings over a timespan of nearly 40 years.

♦ A man living alone was unhappy. Then he met a woman. Then, as a result, he was happy.

While all three of these examples are narratives in that they contain a sequence of events, only the third is a minimal story. But, you may argue, it's not even interesting. Perhaps not. However, as the Routledge *Encyclopedia of Narrative* explains, the physical happenings in a story must be associated with mental states and events such as goals, plans and emotions. Changes in the former affect the latter. Only the third example has this dynamic.

The first story is an anecdote, an ironic happening that is not dependent on the character's mental state for its effect. The second is an intriguing situation, but there's no mention of any mental state, either static or changed. By contrast, our final example involves a major transition from one emotional state to another, with 'happy' being the inverse of 'unhappy'. And what triggers that transition? Yes, it's a specific event, the meeting between the man and the woman.

Here in miniature, then, is a three-link progression that you will find in countless successful stories, ranging from simple folk tales through magazine fiction to character-driven novels. Indeed, all our third story requires is more detail to make it work.

By taking on board the idea of transition from one emotional state to another, triggered by a specific event, you open the door to an infinite variety of stories. You also begin to appreciate why descriptions of dreams and reminiscences, however detailed or elegantly written, are invariably returned with 'not suitable for our market' scrawled on their rejection slip. This doesn't mean you can't use dreams and reminiscences in your stories. You just need to make sure that they have a role to play in that overall dynamic.

It's a lot easier to construct a minimal story once you've seen how it works and magazine stories are a great resource here. Every story contains one major transition, and they are easy to find because they always occur near the end. Once you've got that, it's a simple enough task to identify what triggered that transition.

Let's look at an example. In Rachel Lovell's *The Problem with Mary,* published in *Take a Break* magazine, the main character is a mother who's disappointed in her daughter Mary. She had wanted a *normal* daughter but Mary is a dropout who left school at 16, saying she didn't have time for exams. So, disappointment is the character's initial state. That needs to change.

The event that triggers the transition occurs on a holiday Mary organises for her mother, herself, and Deirdre, who is a disabled woman from the old people's home where Mary works. At first, the mother is irritated by having the holiday spoiled by a third party. She leaves Mary alone and goes off to explore on her own. Later, however, they all meet up by chance when visiting a castle on the tourist trail. Mary is struggling to get Deirdre's wheelchair up the steps so Deirdre can enjoy the view. When the mother sees Deirdre's gratitude to Mary, she begins to see Mary in a different light. Here is the transition, written in the first person from the mother's point of view.

> *'She's wonderful is your Mary.' Tears sparkled in Deirdre's eyes as she held onto Mary, like a drowning man. 'Wonderful. That's what she is.'*
>
> *Tears began to prick at my eyes too. Tears of pride. 'She is,' I said, finding it difficult to speak. 'She's special.'*

So there you are. I'm sure it took Rachel Lovell a lot longer than five minutes to write her story, but as I hope you can see, there is a minimal structure at its heart. We can express it quite simply as:

A mother is disappointed in her daughter. This disappointment changes to pride when she sees her daughter's ability to make other people happy.

Now, have a go at the exercise.

THE EXERCISE

Choose just one of the following emotional states and write a minimal story, making sure you include both a transition from one state to another and a trigger for that transition.

Note that although the two states don't have to be opposites, they should be on the same continuum. So, for example, you could have an unhappy character moving closer to the 'happy' end of the continuum, but you might have a problem if he switched from unhappiness to surprise.

anger	guilt	sadness
anxiety	hate	shame
despair	hopelessness	worry
indecision	hostility	loneliness
fear	jealousy	disappointment
grief	suspicion	

Alternatively, choose your own state(s).

For a Satisfying Ending,
Try a Tin of Magnolia

Having trouble with endings? You're not alone. Writing fiction is all about creating problems and challenges for our characters, but sooner or later, the story has to end. That can be one big headache for the tyro writer. This is because most beginners start with short stories in which that last 'bite of the apple' is proportionately more important. In fact, many new writers' stories don't really have a middle because by the time the writer has set out the problem, she's so desperate to solve it that she bolts for the end like a runaway horse. The result is too often a contrived ending that leaves the reader feeling let down.

If this is you, relax. You don't have to solve everything in a short story.

Let me explain. If you've read Exercise 46, you'll know that the most important thing in any story is change. If characters are able to see that possibility for change, they can head off paddling in the right direction. Instead of thinking major change, think small. The experience of novelist Denise Robertson is a wonderful example of 'thinking small'. In 1978, Robertson and her family had to downsize after her husband's building business went into liquidation. Times were tough, but Robertson, who was a new writer at the time, was determined to make the best of it. In an article entitled 'An end of agony at this healing house', Robertson describes the family's move to a small Durham red-brick house which, 'gave us back everything we had lost.' She writes:

> *It was a lovely Victorian terrace that had been abused. One of my first jobs was picking up rocks that had gone through the window. One room was painted khaki, another black, the bedroom was magenta. My husband's dole was £19 a week, so I could only afford one tin of magnolia paint. Gradually, a tin at a time, I spread a tide of magnolia through the place.*

I love this story. In fiction, as in the real world, there are rarely pat solutions but that doesn't mean that writers have to send in the SAS or a rich uncle to rescue characters in trouble. They're not powerless. As the old Chinese proverb says: 'A journey of a thousand miles begins with a single step'. So, next time your characters are stuck in problem city, remember that tin of magnolia paint. It's a good writing metaphor. And speaking of metaphors, try this exercise.

THE EXERCISE

The following list of words all have metaphorical meaning in terms of negotiating challenges and moving beyond boundaries, either real or imagined, which is, in the end, what stories and life are all about. For example, we talk of turning the corner, seeing a window of opportunity, and so on. This exercise is not about coining metaphors but of taking words and using them to open metaphorical doors in your imagination. Pick a word and freewrite for five minutes.

corner

window

door

gate

mountain

ladder

river

staircase

carpet (think magic)

key

48

How to Plump Up 'Thin' Characters

The 'thin' or 'flat' character is a common problem with a simple
root cause. Either the writer doesn't know the character, or s/he
isn't using what s/he does know in a way that brings out the
character's individuality. Sometimes, characters will show you the
way if you let them – check out the character whisperer exercise
on page 76. However, if you don't really know who your character
is or what they're about, it's time to go back and do a little
homework.

According to an ancient African proverb, 'It takes a village to
raise a child', meaning that as we grow up we are shaped and
influenced by the people around us. In writing classes, we do a
character-creation exercise that incorporates this idea in a group-
brainstorming approach. To begin, each student thinks up the
name and age of a character and writes these down at the top of a
sheet of paper. Each sheet then gets passed to the next person
who reads the name and adds another detail to the character.
And so on. We usually work through a set list of questions, such
as 'What does this character do when they're feeling angry?' or
'To whom does this character turn when they're upset?'

Finally, each paper is returned to its original owner who uses the
answers to write a character analysis. The idea here is that when
20 people all contribute something different to a character, it
gives the original creator of that character a lot to think about. It
doesn't matter if the writer then goes on to scrap some – or even

all – of the details and replace them with others. What matters is the thinking through, the answering of tricky questions. In the end, 'plump' characters are those who are alive for the writer outside the confines of the story and that can only happen if the author is prepared to do a bit of digging.

This may sound obvious. However, in writing classes I have found that there are always one or two students who actively erect barriers between themselves and their characters. One striking example of such a barrier occurred when a student handed me his character sheet after completing the above class exercise. The name, he told me, was a 'cover' identity for a secret service agent. That's fine as far as it goes. However this student had then interpreted all the lovely details on the sheet as applying to the cover personality. The result was that he had learned absolutely nothing about the actual character. If you don't know your character, neither can the reader.

Below, you'll find a list of ideas and questions that have worked well in classes. If you belong to a writers' circle, you might like to use them in a group exercise. Eventually, though, it's good to use on your own.

THE EXERCISE

First, write down a name and age at the top of your sheet of paper. If this is a group exercise, pass this to the person sitting on your right. (The person on your left will now pass their name and age to you.) And so on as each fresh detail is added. If you're on your own, simply respond to as many of the following prompts as you can in five minutes:

◆ To whom does your character turn for advice?

◆ What are your character's 'hidden' attributes, meaning those known to the character but which the character would prefer others not to know?

◆ What are your character's 'blind' attributes, meaning those others can see but of which the character is unaware? (Remember, these could be positive or negative.)

◆ Identify a frightening situation or moment from your character's childhood.

◆ With whom does your character feel most relaxed or at ease?

◆ What is your character's driving force in life?

◆ What is the first thing other people notice about your character? Note that this doesn't have to be something visual.

◆ Who is your character's best friend?

◆ Name one incident or event your character would prefer to forget.

◆ In close relationships, is your character more likely to be the comforter or the comforted?

◆ When your character is angry, how does s/he express it? (Note, if s/he doesn't get angry, what does s/he do instead?)

◆ Is your character a spender or a saver?

◆ What is your character's weakness?

◆ What is your character's relationship to food? (For example, where, when, and what do they eat? Are they overweight?)

◆ What 'mask' or 'masks' does your character wear? (For example, does your character hide feelings behind a 'happy' face?)

◆ What music does your character like?

Once you have your list of answers, freewrite a piece about your character, using the collected information as inspiration. My students refer to this as a character 'ramble' and that's exactly what it is. It's not designed for publication, so you can forget style and grammar. Just write.

Remember, too, that you can add or delete questions to create a dossier tailored to the kind of fiction you want to write. If you're into romance, for example, you might want to include your character's idea of the perfect partner. For thrillers, it might be useful to know your character's deepest fear. Feel free to throw in a few wild cards, such as your character's attitude to buying presents for people. According to Jeremy Clarkson, for example, his Christmas gift-giving is entirely dependent on what he can find within 30ft of whatever Harrods' door he's been able to park outside. That tells us a lot about his income, social status, and personality.

49

Please Insert Address

Have you ever noticed how volume house builders strive to give their new developments beautiful names? I once bought a small house off-plan in a brick and concrete maze known as Badgers Copse. I never saw any badgers and the only copse was a spindly sapling on everyone's front lawn. That didn't stop the developers creating addresses designed to lead us all up a nostalgia cul-de-sac. There was a Briar Walk, a Cherry Tree Close, a Maple Grove. None of these roads had any actual trees.

Nowadays, apartments have been hauled onto the bandwagon. You want grand? Try The Chatsworth or The Buckingham. Or perhaps you prefer the Wisteria Lane charm of ABC's *Desperate Housewives*. You'll be dazzled by The Cape Cod. When you move in, or course, you'll be hard pressed to see any significant difference between one style and another, apart from the facade. Inside is just a box and a flat-pack kitchen in your preferred flavour. It's a cosmetic illusion, so why does it work?

It works because what the developers are selling you is a prime cut of your own imagination. As Dee Hawkins, interior designer for a major house builder explains on her company's website: 'In show houses we are selling a dream and an ideal.' In fact, the dream starts with the address. For example, while Tyre Factory Lane immediately sounds smelly and noisy, Spring Valley conjures up images of flowers and rolling meadows. First impressions die hard. Consequently, creating an address for a character is a powerful way to kick-start both your reader's imagination and your own. Consider Daphne du Maurier's *Jamaica Inn*, Harold Robbins' *79, Park Avenue*, or Sebastian Faulks' *On Green Dolphin Street*. These books *sound* interesting, yet all we know about them is where they take place.

When you add a specific character, you can increase the interest level even more, as Dee Williams does in her historical sagas set in London's East End. There is *Carrie of Culver Road, Hannah of Hope Street, Annie of Albert Mews.* Lucy Maud Montgomery used this technique for her classic series beginning with *Anne of Green Gables,* as did Helene Hanff for *The Duchess of Bloomsbury Street,* her sequel to the fantastically successful *84, Charing Cross Road.* Consider, too, how the character and the address might interact on a symbolic level. For example, where 'Duchess' and 'Bloomsbury' create an atmosphere of literary tradition with a touch of celebrity, the flavour of Eve Garnett's *The Family from One End Street* sounds altogether more cosy and comfortable.

Experiment with ideas in the following exercise.

THE EXERCISE

◆ Create a variety of different street addresses. Of course, there's no need to stick with streets. You can include roads, lanes, closes, courts, groves, buildings, or whatever else that takes your fancy. Short of inspiration? Look at a map, or simply note down the roads you pass when you're out in your car or on public transport.

◆ Take a single road – real or imaginary – and start to compile a list of the different people who might live there. For example, Green Pond Lane is a street I drive past quite frequently on my way between Winchester and Romsey. I don't know anyone there but I like the sound of the name and that's a good start. Who lives at number 22? I don't actually know if there *is* a number 22, but that's all to the good. I can have fun imagining a polished oak door with a neat porch and maybe a potted bay tree that needs watering. In my mind, I see the door opening and a woman coming out. She's young, wearing a bright print skirt and a short jacket. Her name is … Natasha, but her friends call her Tashi. Now, who lives next door? And so on.

TIP: If you're fed up with your own country's addresses, try somewhere abroad. The Internet has brought maps of almost anywhere within easy grasp, and the same goes for telephone directories. Australia and America, for example, both have *White Pages* online, and you can spend a very enjoyable five minutes keying in common surnames (try Brown) and an initial, to see what comes up. Using this strategy, I came up with Mandalay Street, in Fig Tree Pocket, Queensland, which has to be one of the loveliest addresses on the planet.

50

What Does This Feel Like?

There are a myriad ways to get a story on the road and I am constantly fascinated by authors' tales of what first inspires them. In this book, I've tried to cover as many as I can, but there are always more. Just today, I came across an interview with Joanna Trollope on her publisher's website. Trollope's novels have all been published by Transworld under its Black Swan imprint, and you can find links to other author interviews on the same site. While many authors like to start with character or place, Trollope says that, for her, the idea comes first. She favours emotional situations that pose some kind of dilemma but whatever it is, it must be able to answer the question: what does it feel like? For example, 'What does it feel like to be married to someone else's vocation? What does it feel like to go through a complicated grief? What does it feel like to be the child of a broken marriage, to be single at 30, to fall in love with your stepmother …?'

Trollope fans may recognise these ideas in the plots of her published novels, but for Trollope, this is a very fluid stage of creation. If an idea seems promising, she says, she starts a notebook into which she pastes bits of information she thinks might be useful – 'flotsam and jetsam' – until a story begins to emerge.

Similarly, Anne Cassidy, who writes thrillers and murder mystery novels for teenagers, finds that exploring her main character's feelings helps her to get her books up and running. In *Missing*

Judy, for example, she created a family whose daughter has gone missing. However, instead of focusing on the missing girl, she looked at the sibling who'd been left behind. What, she wondered, might it feel like to be the brother or sister of that missing child? In *Looking for JJ,* she wanted to explore the disturbing world of children who kill, choosing as her main character a girl sent to prison for murdering her friend. As you can imagine, this was by no means an easy book to write – it's all too easy just to demonise the child. But Cassidy didn't do this. Instead, she tried to imagine how the girl might feel when released from prison, having served her term. Could she ever forget the past? Could she forgive herself? And so on. The method worked for Cassidy and for readers, too. *Looking for JJ* went on to win the Booktrust Teenage Book Award, and was shortlisted for many more.

In writers' workshops, we often use this method to generate a pool of useful triggers for students to dip into, whatever their metier. It works for all kinds of stories, articles and even poems. Try it for yourself.

THE EXERCISE

Make a list, starting with the words 'What does it feel like to …'

Be as imaginative or silly as you like. I don't know what inspired Stephen Chbosky to write his controversial coming-of-age novel *The Perks of Being a Wallflower,* but one thing's for sure. Before he could write it, he first had to ask himself, 'What does it feel like?'

Come up with as many ideas as you can. Later, choose just one of your triggers to write a longer piece.

Food for Thought

---

*When Sean Devine and Jimmy Marcus were kids, their
fathers worked together at the Coleman Candy plant and
carried the stench of warm chocolate back home with them. It
became a permanent character of their clothes, the beds they
slept in, the vinyl backs of their car seats. Sean's kitchen
smelled like a Fudgsicle, his bathroom like a Coleman Chew-
Chew bar. By the time they were eleven, Sean and Jimmy had
developed a hatred of sweets so total that they took their
coffee black for the rest of their lives and never ate dessert.*

Dennis Lehane, *Mystic River*

As adults, our relationship with food is a complex one that begins
as soon as we are born. Because this relationship is both primeval
and social, everyone can relate to fiction that uses food to
establish its characters. In the above extract from his tough thriller
Mystic River, Dennis Lehane uses two boys' early memories of
chocolate to characterise the closeness between them and to
symbolise their shared histories. In the process of reading this,
however, we can smell and taste the chocolate. As a result, we find
ourselves drawn into the story on a sensory level.

It's a neat trick that works for any kind of fiction, both mass-
market and literary. Take, for example, Elizabeth Baines' short
story, *A Glossary of Bread*. First published in the prestigious *Stand
Magazine,* it explores the legacy of exile and racial prejudice
through the eyes of a child. With a lot to say in a limited space,

Baines cleverly uses the different breads – rolls, baps, barn cakes and muffins – as a means of linking the child's disparate memories of growing up. The story has since been published online at: *www.eastoftheweb.com/short-stories/UBooks/ GlosBrea.shtml*

In real life, food has both immediate and nostalgic resonance. This means that we can use it not just to establish our characters' reality, but also to recapture images and incidents from our own past. For some writers, this can be astonishingly effective. In his 3,000-page *Remembrance of Things Past* French novelist Marcel Proust describes how the taste of a cake dipped in tea was sufficient to unlock the memories of his own 'lost' youth:

> *And as soon as I had recognised the taste of the piece of madeleine soaked in her decoction of lime-blossom which my aunt used to give me ... immediately the old grey house upon the street, where her room was, rose up like a stage set to attach itself to the little pavilion opening on to the garden which had been built out behind it for my parents ... and with the house the town, from morning to night and in all weathers, the Square where I used to be sent before lunch, the streets along which I used to run errands, the country roads we took when it was fine.*

For Proust, the tea functions here as a powerful catalyst not just for the immediate memory of tasting the cake but of an emotional past lying dormant, just waiting to be retrieved. In Proust's words, it 'all sprang into being, town, and garden alike, from my cup of tea'. For many writers, such images are the compost from which their fiction springs. As Ray Bradbury wrote in the preface to *Dandelion Wine:* 'I was gathering images all my life, storing them away, and forgetting them. Somehow I had to send myself back ... to open the memories out and see what they had to offer.'

Food is the perfect catalyst because it involves all the senses. We don't just taste food, we see it, smell it, touch it and even hear it. Think of the crunch of apples, the crispy sizzle of bacon, the crack of crème brûlée. In writing classes we often use the following exercise to help students recover their own forgotten images.

THE EXERCISE

What are your food memories? Best-selling author Wendy Holden once described hers as the Mr Whippy ice cream van that used to stop outside her home in Cleckheaton, West Yorkshire. The taste was 'intoxicatingly blended with the fumes from the exhaust'. Make a list of your own food memories, or, if you prefer, do a creative search. Start with your earliest – some of my students remember Farley's rusks – and work forwards. Then, choose one of your memories to write a longer piece.

52

So What Do *You* Do For a Living?

In one of her famous early articles, 'The Glamour of Doctors', Jilly Cooper tells the story of a male friend who was at a party where no one was paying him any attention. He turned to the nearest woman and told her he was a gynaecologist en route to an international fertility conference. This was a lie, but as Cooper explains, it had the desired effect:

> *From that moment on, he was mobbed. All the women crowded round him, bombarding him with questions. One pretty girl insisted he came upstairs and examined her. Two journalists interviewed him and a TV producer offered him airspace.*

OK, so some occupations just happen to have more fascination-value than others and it's well worth bearing this in mind when you're creating your characters. Doctors, nurses and vets have long been safe bets, as have police officers and private eyes, but there are plenty of other intriguing occupations, so why stick with the bland and obvious? This is one great way to add colour to your characters. Imagine you've just arrived at a party and the hostess offers to introduce you to either a clerical worker for the gas board or a chocolatier. Hard choice, huh? My guess is you'll go for the chocolatier.

Similarly, in fiction, choose wisely and you'll not only have a more interesting character but a greater variety of plot ideas, too. Susan Orlean's *The Orchid Thief* is a striking example of a non-fiction book whose central figure, John Laroche, is so mesmerising that Columbia Pictures signed up writer Charlie Kauffman to adapt it for the screen:

> *John Laroche is a tall guy, skinny as a stick, pale-eyed, slouch-shouldered, and sharply handsome, in spite of the fact that he is missing all his front teeth. He has the posture of al dente spaghetti and the nervous intensity of someone who plays a lot of video games.*

But what makes Laroche so fascinating is his occupation as a plant dealer and his obsessive search for rare orchids. Indeed, so passionate is he about orchids that he was once arrested for stealing protected species from the Fakahatchee Strand, a nature reserve in south Florida. Although Orlean's book has no real plot, Kauffman created one for the film using the orchid thief's world of passion and obsession to fuel his ideas.

An unusual occupation is also useful in genre fiction where writers are constantly looking for a fresh slant on old themes. As the Romantic Times Book Club explains on its website, the occupation of a main character normally plays a central role in developing conflict.

> *If the hero is a tornado chaser, the heroine might enter his life as a social worker concerned about the effects of his dangerous job on his child. If the heroine is a landscape designer, the hero might very likely be Mr. Rich Property owner who can't believe any woman can do the job he requires. Perhaps hero and heroine are competitors in the same field, or sometimes the hero's work (soldier of fortune,*

secret agent, gambler) entangles the heroine in entirely new adventures.

The great thing about giving a character an unusual job is that it gives you the chance to research it. That research will drip feed your creative well and open doors to new thoughts. For example, I once wrote a short story in which a woman accountant and a male sheep-farmer cross paths. Having once done temporary work in an accountant's office, I was reasonably familiar with balance sheets and VAT, but I knew absolutely nothing about rearing sheep. A couple of books from my local library soon fixed that. After reading them both, I had more than enough material to have my townie accountant floundering in the farmyard. The story, *Counting Sheep*, sold to a national woman's magazine.

Nowadays, of course, the Internet is a vast first-stop resource for anyone curious about the nitty-gritty of particular occupations, with many sites aimed at people looking for a career change. *AirlineCareer.com* will tell you exactly what it's like to be a flight attendant, including first-hand articles about your working day, how to treat celebrities and so on. Or perhaps you're wondering what it takes to be a professional poker player? Check out *www.professional-poker.com* for rules, strategies and famous player profiles. Fancy yourself as a knife thrower? Try *www.knifethrowing. info/index.html*

What you learn will help you to bring a character to life, provided of course that you've got more than just factual information. First-person pieces will normally contain a sprinkling of anecdotes and they're invaluable for giving you a feel for what it's actually like to do the job. In the meantime, try the following exercises.

♦ Make a list of all the jobs that you've had. Include holiday work, temporary work and anything you've ever tried, even for just a day. Include jobs you've liked, and ones that you've hated.

♦ Go through your list and select one job for use in a creative search or a five-minute freewrite.

♦ Write a list of dream jobs – and then research your favourite to find out exactly what it involves.

♦ Write a list of the most unusual jobs you can think of. And if you can't think of any, check out *Odd Jobs: Portraits of Unusual Occupations* by Nancy Rica Schiff.

53

We're All Part of a System

When I was working as a couple counsellor, I was trained to see the couple not just as individuals but as part of a 'system', a network of social and cultural influences that includes family, friends, work and even the media. This 'systemic' approach is based on the idea that people develop through interactions with others, starting with the first relationship between a baby and its caregiver. Consequently, when something goes wrong in a relationship – any relationship – the key to fixing it often depends on understanding the system in which it is embedded. Actions are never isolated. They are always reactions to something else. As psychologist Lynne Namka explains:

> *Members of a system are like the moving pieces of a mobile. The behaviour of one person in the system affects the others just as touching one object of a mobile sets the whole system moving.*

What has this to do with writing fiction? Everything. Too many beginners' stories fail because readers only see the characters strutting their stuff in one part of the 'system'. That's not how real people live their lives. Real people have to exist in multiple compartments, and problems in one seep through to the others. This results in conflicting demands on the individual's time and emotional resources.

When readers are not privy to this systemic seepage, the character will seem flat. This can easily happen if, for example, the character is so busy pursuing a goal that readers learn nothing of other areas of the character's life. Imagine what your own life would be like if you had only one relationship to consider. Most of us have to multitask on this emotional level, balancing our commitments to work, home, social life, and so on. Consequently, one of the easiest ways to counteract thin characters in fiction is to give them a family or a family substitute.

This doesn't mean you have to write a family story. Rather, it means that you will use the 'family' to complicate your characters' lives. Michael Crichton's *Rising Sun,* is a good example of this technique. It's a thriller, set in the world of international finance, but it begins at home. Special services police detective Pete Smith is learning Japanese from a language tape while his two-year-old daughter sleeps:

> *I had my textbook open on the bed, alongside a Mr Potato Head I'd put back together for my daughter. Next to that, a photo album, and the pictures from her second birthday party. It was four months after Michelle's party, but I still put the pictures in the album. You have to try and keep up with that stuff ... The pictures on my bed didn't reflect reality any more. Four months later, Michelle looked completely different. She was taller; she'd outgrown the expensive party dress my ex-wife had bought for her: black velvet with a white lace collar.*

What readers learn here about Peter helps them to empathise with him. Mr Potato Head and the photo album show us he's a loving dad. He's conscientious: *You have to try and keep up with that stuff*. He's also acutely aware of how fast children change. Every parent in the world can identify with that. And he's a single father. Throughout the novel, Peter continues to care for his daughter, cooking pancakes for her when he's at home, making her bed, protecting her when danger threatens. This sub-plot exists alongside the main one, showing us another side to Peter, and one to which we can wholeheartedly relate. As a result, Peter is a far more authentic character then he could possibly be if Crichton had shown him existing in a work capacity only.

THE EXERCISE

Imagine that your character is coming home from work, thinking about the different areas of their life. Now, write a quick sub-plot episode to illustrate just one of those areas. Remember that a sub-plot isn't simply a different viewpoint on the main events. It's another dimension of the character's life, one which is the source of a secondary problem or goal. For example, your character might have to cope with an ageing parent whose health has suddenly taken a turn for the worse, a teenage son or daughter who's mixing with the wrong crowd, an alcoholic sibling, or even a problematic pet. Don't bother to explain the problem; just dive straight in as Crichton has done with Pete Smith, charting the immediate thoughts tumbling through the character's mind.

What Do You Want ... Really?

Early in the writing workshop year, I always set my students this exercise, not because I'm a nosey-parker but because desire – for achievement, love, survival, whatever – is the driving force of fiction. To paraphrase Aristotle, we *are* our desires. Without desire, we have no motivation to do anything, and stories without desire are mostly too dull to publish. Consciously or unconsciously, we all strive to actualise our desires and the way we choose to do so reveals us as people. For example, many of us would like to be free of financial worries, but how do we achieve this? One person may buy a lottery ticket. Another may work around the clock. Another may buy into a risky get-rich-quick scheme.

In real life, desire shapes our destiny. The man who works around the clock may come home to find his partner has left him for someone more attentive. The lottery ticket buyer may go to the same shop every week and strike up an acquaintance with the person behind the counter. The get-rich-quick schemer may start borrowing from relatives, and end up with debts he or she can't pay off. And so on. In fiction, as in life, desire shapes the possibilities of our story. And in this respect, what a character wants is less important than how much they want it. The more desperately a character wants something, the more he or she will be driven to act. That's what keeps the plot interesting and the story alive.

Before we can write about our characters' wants and desires, however, we need first to acknowledge our own. Some students have amazing difficulty with this. They struggle to find laudable wants: world peace, perhaps, or an end to human suffering. This is understandable. We want to be seen as 'good' people. But the truth is that most fiction tends to germinate in rather less altruistic soil. It is peopled by characters on a voyage of self-discovery, or in some cases, self-destruction. Think of Macbeth, who so wants to be king that he murders his best friend.

But you don't need to act like Macbeth to desire things you can't have. And part of the appeal of both reading and writing fiction is exploring those desires. Go ahead; try the following exercise.

THE EXERCISE

I want ...

List ten things you want now, or have ever wanted, in your lifetime. Try to include a mixture of big, small and even frivolous things. Also include things that you know — for whatever reason — are impossible. One of my students wrote a poem about the things he most wanted, finishing with the realisation that although he knew they were pipe-dreams, they were still *his* dreams. The sour-sweet nature of the poem earned him a prize in a regional contest.

Opposition Creates Meaning

Have you ever stopped to consider how much of our everyday language consists of contrasts or opposites? 'How're things?' someone asks us. 'Oh, you know, up and down,' we reply. 'Brrr, it's cold today.' 'Yes, but I hear it'll be warm tomorrow.'

Opposition creeps into advertising: 'Soft ice cream encased in crunchy nut chocolate.' It even appears in the titles of our fiction. *Beauty and the Beast*, *The Prince and the Pauper*, *Snow White and Rose Red*.

According to Swiss linguist Ferdinand de Saussure and French anthropologist Claude Lévi-Strauss, this is no accident. Our world is based on binary oppositions – night and day, left and right, nature and culture – and these oppositions are essential to our understanding. In other words, we don't derive meaning from what things *are*, but from their relationship to other things. How, for example, could we explain the meaning of 'rich' without the concept of 'poor'? Similarly, top has no meaning without bottom, life without death, male without female.

This is powerful stuff but it doesn't stop there. Many story analysts argue that opposition or contrast is fundamental to our understanding of narrative. Lévi-Strauss, for example, asks us to consider why myths, legends and folk tales have universal resonance, despite wide cultural differences in their content and characters. The answer, he argues, is in their structural similarities. Take any myth, reduce it to its smallest component parts and you will find a series of binary oppositions – or paired contrasts.

We don't have to look very far to establish the truth of this. In all traditional tales, you will find heroes and villains, allies and enemies, goals and obstacles, strength and weakness, justice and injustice – to name just a few. We take many of these oppositions for granted, and when they are missing – as in a beginner's story, perhaps – we're left wondering what sense we are to make of it. Myth, then, is a language, a universal narrative that transcends cultural and historical boundaries to speak to us all.

If we want to write engaging fiction, we, too, need to consider using oppositions. This is because all successful stories hark back to myth. Hands up those who enjoy reading crime novels? In a recent article in *The Observer* colour supplement, French writer Fred Vargas argues that the appeal of such stories is their similarity to fairytales. (Vargas novels translated into English include *Have Mercy On Us All* and *Seeking Whom He May Devour*.) The murderer is the dragon, while the detectives are knights in armour who must find their way through the dark forest. They are, she says 'the stories we tell ourselves to survive, or to live better, or to explain the dangers in life. It's only by facing the threats that we discover how to go on.'

Oppositions can work at different levels. At a deep level, you might find something like good versus evil, an opposition that has an infinite number of variations. On a more explicit level, it could be two characters whose looks are very different. Here, for example, is how Ruth Rendell introduces Inspectors Wexford and Burden in *Means of Evil*:

Wexford, getting on for sixty, was a tall, ungainly, rather ugly man who had once been fat to the point of obesity but had slimmed to gauntness for reasons of health. Nearly twenty years his junior, Burden had the slenderness of a man who has always been thin. His face was ascetic, handsome in a frosty way. The older man, who had a good wife who looked after him devotedly, nevertheless always looked as if his clothes came off the peg from the War on Want Shop, while the younger, a widower, was sartorially immaculate.

You might notice here how the appearance of the characters mirrors a more fundamental opposition, that of care and neglect. There is also health/illness, love/lack of love, married/single, beauty/ugliness – and all in one paragraph.

At first glance, there's nothing particularly deep about James Bond novels. However, could it be that at least part of their phenomenal success might be due to Ian Fleming's prolific use of mythic technique? According to Umberto Eco, in *The Role of the Reader,* all Fleming's novels are 'built on a series of oppositions which allow a limited number of permutations and interactions'. Some of these are opposing character pairings, including Bond/villain, woman/Bond. Others are opposing values such as duty/sacrifice, luxury/discomfort, loyalty/disloyalty, which the various characters personify throughout the story. These oppositions occur in all Bond stories and, as Eco points out, they are universal. Take luxury/discomfort, for example. Specific definitions of both vary wildly but what we all understand is the contrast between the two.

If you want to include binary oppositions in your stories, one of the best ways to start is with character. Put the character or characters in a scene that illustrates the opposition. In the classic film *The African Queen,* for example, nature and civilisation is an ongoing theme, with Humphrey Bogart (Charlie Allnut) characterising the former and Katherine Hepburn (Rose Sayer) the latter. In one great scene, Bogart, an uncouth drifter who owns his own boat, delivers mail to Hepburn, who is working as a missionary in German East Africa at the beginning of the First World War. As they sit, taking tea, the unshaven Bogart is suffering from trapped wind and his stomach keeps rumbling. Hepburn, dressed in high neck and long sleeves despite the heat, pours the tea into china cups. She ignores Bogart's embarrassed efforts to apologise. 'Have a rock cake, Mr Allnut,' she smiles, as if this were 4 o'clock in middle England.

How can characters from such different backgrounds possibly learn to communicate on equal ground? You'll have to watch the film for that. In the meantime, try the following exercise.

THE EXERCISE

Choose an opposition from the list, then either plan or write a short scene, using one or two characters to personify the opposing ideas.

past/future	inside/outside
excess/moderation	beauty/ugliness
good/bad	town/country
passive/active	youth/old age
rich/poor	dependence/independence
self/other	strength/weakness

56

The Age of Epiphany

The great Raymond Carver used to scribble useful bits of information on three-by-five cards which he then taped to the wall beside his desk. One featured a fragment of a sentence by Chekhov. Carver writes:

'... and suddenly everything became clear to him.' I find these words filled with wonder and possibility. I love their simple clarity, and the hint of revelation that is implied. There is a bit of mystery, too. What has been unclear before? Why is it just now becoming clear? What's happened? Most of all – what now? There are consequences as a result of such sudden awakenings.

That 'sudden awakening' or 'epiphany', as James Joyce called it, is the bit in a story that makes everything else slot into place. It is the *why* of the narrative, its reason for being, as opposed to the *what next?* It is one of the things that raises story above anecdote and leaves readers feeling that something has been resolved.

Perhaps one of the most famous examples of epiphany occurs at the end of the film *Casablanca,* when Rick gives up Ilse, the woman he loves. 'If that plane leaves the ground and you're not on it, you'll regret it,' he tells her. 'Maybe not tonight. Maybe not tomorrow. But someday and for the rest of your life.'

Rick has realised that we can't always just take what we want. Every action has consequences and sometimes it's better to look at the bigger picture, the 'hill of beans'. Ilse has a husband, war hero Viktor Lazlo, who loves her and needs her. It may not be the heady romance that Rick and Ilse shared but as Rick tells Ilse: 'We'll always have Paris.'

Ilse gets on the plane. The love triangle is resolved.

Of course, epiphanies come in many flavours. In a magazine story, which caters for a family market, it may be a mother's sudden realisation that a child needs its own space, that an interfering in-law is desperate to be liked, or that you don't have to be perfect to be loved. What is important is that the writer shows what led up to the epiphany. One of my students read out a story that finished with the line *At first she had blamed him for the accident and now she didn't.*

What are we supposed to make of this? I asked the writer to explain, but all he could do was shrug. 'Maybe,' he said eventually, 'she realises it wasn't his fault. I'm sure the intelligent reader can work it out.'

The student seemed to be asking the readers to write the story themselves. This is dangerous practice. Stories are not about testing the reader's intelligence. They are about opening windows in the mind. If you like the idea of pulling something out of a hat, make it a rabbit, not an epiphany.

We all have epiphanic moments in our lives. Some happen in a flash, like a ray of sunshine from behind a cloud. Some take time and the path that leads to them is strewn with brambles and potholes. When one does happen, though, it changes your way of thinking forever. Once you know about sex, for example, there is no going back to childhood innocence. In this respect, you might like to think of epiphany as an awakening, a new way of seeing the world, or at least your own small piece of it. Sometimes, that's a positive thing. Sometimes, it's sad. Sometimes – and this often makes for very powerful fiction, it's both sweet and sour. Try the following exercise.

THE EXERCISE

Make a list of your own epiphanic moments, good, bad and sweet-sour. Include large ones and small ones. If you once believed in Santa Claus, for example, when and how did you discover he didn't exist? When you've finished your list, choose one to write about in more detail in another session.

Setting As Character

Herr Koch led the way into the flat that had been Harry's. In the little dark hall there was still the smell of cigarette smoke – the Turkish cigarettes that Harry always smoked. It seemed odd that a man's smell should cling in the folds of curtains so long after the man himself had become dead matter, a gas, a decay. One light, in a heavily beaded shade, left them in semi-darkness, fumbling for door handles.

Graham Greene, *The Third Man*

When you want to describe a character, you probably don't immediately think of setting. Yet psychological research shows that the spaces we inhabit – our homes and our work environments – offer rich and accurate information about the kind of people we are. A study in *The Journal of Personality and Social Psychology* identified four key mechanisms we use to imprint ourselves, both consciously and unconsciously, on our personal space (Gosling *et al.* (2002) 'A room with a cue: personality judgements based on offices and bedrooms').

First off, there are *self-directed identity claims,* symbolic statements that are intended to 'reinforce' the view that people already have of themselves. These include personal choice of decoration and memorabilia such as a pebble collected from a favourite beach, or other objects of sentimental value. Then there are *other-directed identity claims,* things that people use deliberately to communicate their attitudes or values to others.

These often have a shared meaning, such as a poster indicating that the occupant supports this or that cause, or is a fan of a particular film or pop star.

After this comes *interior behavioural residue,* which refers to the physical traces of how we live our lives. In the above extract from *The Third Man,* the smell of Harry's cigarette smoke is behavioural residue. A pile of empty wine bottles in the kitchen is behavioural residue, as is an alphabetised CD collection, or neat stack of ironing in the airing cupboard. By contrast, *exterior behavioural residue* refers to things we do outside our living space. That might include things like sporting equipment, holiday photos, or even a used bus ticket.

When we use such physical cues and clues in our fiction, we're showing the readers who the characters are. Readers pick up the details and use them to construct their own image of the character's personality. To avoid stereotyping, introduce contrast. For example, what would you expect a writer of erotic literature to have on her desk? An Ann Summers catalogue? The *Kama Sutra?* Mitzi Szereto, whose latest book is *In Sleeping Beauty's Bed*, reveals that she keeps a bowl of sweets on hers, either liquorice toffees or a bag of wine gums – and a purple eraser.

THE EXERCISES

1. Think about your own home. What does it reveal about you? Make a list, including at least one item from each of the four key mechanisms (self and other identity claims; interior and exterior behavioural residue).

2. Create a setting with cues to its absent occupier's personality. Write a description of the setting, bringing the absent occupier to life using items from the four key mechanisms.

3. Design a character-revealing living space for one of the following:

   a teenager with low self-esteem

   a 30-something city woman

   a single man with no plans to settle down

   a grandparent

   a low-income person with high aspirations

   a person in poor health.

Decisions, Decisions

Have you ever wondered how many decisions you make in a day? Fifty? A hundred? A study published by the magazine *Environment and Behaviour* found that the average person makes well over 200 decisions a day about food alone. When you add decisions about what to wear, whether to collect your dry-cleaning at lunchtime or wait until later when the shop might be closed, who to call about the broken thingy on the washing machine, life begins to sound like one long dilemma. That's before you've even started on the difficult stuff like whether you should change your job or move to Australia.

With so much practice, you'd think we'd all be expert decision-makers, but here's the funny thing. Many of us still find it difficult to make up our minds. In one of my recent writing classes, for example, not a single person claimed to find decision-making easy. The class included a project manager, a finance officer and someone running their own business.

They're not unusual. Some of the most successful individuals, people we trust to make decisions affecting national and international security, have the same problem. In the 1980s, for example, Americans were shocked to discover that ex-President Reagan, once the most powerful man in the world, had consulted his wife's astrologer to help him plan the White House Diary. Closer to home, former Chanel model Elizabeth Teissier caused a stir in France when it was reported she'd been an astrological advisor to President Mitterand. She even wrote a book about it: *Sous le Signe de Mitterand* (Under the Sign of Mitterand).

Scary, huh? Scary, too, is the realisation that even when we think we're making a rational decision, we're probably deluding ourselves. According to researchers at the Max Planck Institute of Cognitive Science in Leipzig, it's our unconscious that makes the decisions. Using an MRI scanner to monitor signals in the brain, researchers found they could predict someone's decision up to ten seconds before the participant was aware of having made it.

'It seems that your brain starts to trigger your decision before you make up your mind,' said Dr John-Dylan Haynes, leader of the study. 'We can't rule out free will, but I think it's very implausible.'

Crikey, anyone for tarot? But it doesn't end there. Even when we've made a decision, how do we know it's the right one? Choice always involves consequences, some of which only become apparent over time. If you're interested in reading about some of the world's worst blunders, including corporate chicanery, poor military decisions, and engineering disasters, check out *History's Worst Decisions: An Encyclopedia Idiotica* by Stephen Weir.

So, it's all a bit tricky. No wonder that fear of making a mistake sometimes makes us freeze. But this is good news for fiction writers. Fiction taps into this cognitive pickle by putting characters into situations where decisions are unavoidable. Through fictional characters, we gain vicarious access to roads we might never be able to explore in the real world: the risky roads, the escape roads, the roads into fantasy where anything is possible. When characters make mistakes, it only adds to the conflict, heightens the tension. Part of the pleasure of reading is identifying with characters who can't see ahead but still have to act.

This is neatly articulated in the following extract from Philip Pullman's *The Amber Spyglass,* the final book in *His Dark Materials* trilogy. To put it in context, Will found his father dying at the end of *The Subtle Knife.* Now, he is alone at the top of a mountain, trying to decide what to do next. He promised his father that he would take the knife to Lord Asriel. The angels are also urging him to do this. However, Lyra is missing, abducted by Mrs Coulter. Will is desperate to find her:

Will considered what to do. When you choose one way out of many, all the ways you don't take are snuffed out like candles, as if they'd never existed. At the moment, all Will's choices existed at once. But to keep them all in existence meant doing nothing. He had to choose, after all.

Indeed he does have to choose. Choice leads to action and both are functions of characters in the 'hero' role. If they refuse, the reader loses connection with them because there's nothing to define who the character is. As Dumbledore says in *Harry Potter and the Chamber of Secrets*: '*It is our choices who show who we really are, far more than our abilities.*'

In *The Amber Spyglass,* Will makes his decision and the story moves on. There are more tough choices ahead, not just for Will but for all the main characters. In Chapter 21, for example, Lyra has to decide whether to stay with her beloved daemon or risk losing him forever in her bid to rescue Roger from the land of the dead. Decisions that involve sacrifice will also involve the reader.

You'll find more about choice and consequence in plot construction in Exercise 39. Right now, use the following exercise to explore your own thoughts about decisions and the decision-making process.

THE EXERCISE

Think about the decisions you've made in our own life. What do you consider to be your best decisions? Your worst? Your most difficult? Your easiest? Write for five minutes.

IDEA: To alert you to the prevalence of decisions in everyday life, try keeping a decision-making diary for a day. When you're conscious of making a decision, make a note of it. For example, you might write: '10.30 am – decided to have a cup of coffee. Decided not to have a square of chocolate.' Don't try to record everything. It's not possible, and you'll drive yourself to drink.

Keep in mind that even small decisions can significantly alter the course of our lives. The BBC's *Dr Who* explored this concept in Episode 11 of Series Four. Entitled *Turn Left*, it's a parallel universe story in which Donna (Catherine Tate) has to decide which way to turn at a road junction. If she chooses to go right, the world will be destroyed. If she chooses left … well you get the idea. Check out the *Dr Who* website at: http://www.bbc.co.uk/doctorwho/s4/episodes/

As an experiment, you might try playing around with your decisions and deliberately changing your mind. For example: '7.30 – decided to ring Jo and go out to see a film. No. Decided instead to ring Natasha because I haven't seen her for a while.' This can be quite heady, but also uncomfortable as you are challenging the decision your unconscious has already made.

SOURCES OF LAST LINES IN EXERCISE 18

Spooky, a short story by David Dean

The Eagle has Landed, Jack Higgins

The Sandcastle, Iris Murdoch

The Grand Babylon Hotel, Arnold Bennett

The Spy who Loved Me, Ian Fleming

Remote Control, Andy McNab

From Hayt to Luff, a short story by Steve Beresford

The Brick Thing, a short story by Jack Frederickson

The House of Stairs, Ruth Rendell

When the Bough Breaks, Jonathan Kellerman